FAITH, H
Room for

"It is with a great deal of pleasure that I write in behalf of the God-inspired work of the Galilean Home Ministries run by Sandy and Jerry Tucker. God has indeed given Sandy and Jerry special talents and abilities to love and take care of the many children under their roof.

"There is no way one can adequately express their dedication, love and hard work in behalf of children whose future would be bleak indeed if they had not been fortunate enough to be placed in the Galilean Home under Jerry and Sandy's care. There is no way an award can do justice to the work they do, but as the years have passed and the national and even international awards have mounted, more and more people recognized the special tasks of Sandy and Jerry Tucker. They deserve every word of praise and I can only add mine, once again, in hopes that the entire world can know of their work.

"The Tuckers are indeed an inspiration to us all."

HAROLD ROGERS, Member of Congress

"Suffer the little children to come unto me (Mark 10:14) shows the deep love of Christ for all, but also applies as well to the founders of, and also the parents of the Galilean Home Ministries, Jerry and Sandy Tucker.

"May God bless the efforts in the writing of this book, *Faith, Hope, And Room For One More.*"

EMMETT LANHAM, Jerry and Sandy's Pastor

"The Galilean Home personifies the Gospel in action. From a few acres of land in rural Kentucky, the Galilean Home is reaching out in Christian love to the world's most important resource _ its children. Jerry and Sandy are truly touching the world for Jesus Christ. Their story is one the world must hear. Their burden is one the world must share."

MICHAEL W. HALEY, Ed.D., President, JSBC

"I firmly believe in the ministry of the Galilean Home, as being a place of love and care. I have seen the children from this home, and you can sense the joy and happiness of being a family that is upon them. Jerry and Sandy have taken the precious commodity of love and filled each child's life with it. Talk to any child there and they will tell you how very much they are loved at the Galilean Home."

DUDLEY SMITH, Singles Ministry Pastor and Singer

"The very essence of Christianity is servanthood. Many in the body of Christ today talk about servanthood, but they don't practice it. Jerry and Sandy Tucker, through the Galilean Home Ministries, prove every day to a skeptical world what the love of Jesus Christ is all about."

DONNIE SWAGGART

"Jerry and Sandy Tucker are ordinary people who live truly on faith, hope, and room for one more.

"I have been amazed at the children's contentment under stressful conditions. The children have come from life threatening and abusive situations, or in such poor physical condition, that their parents couldn't care for them. I believe that it is the unconditional love that Jerry and Sandy have for these children which heals their wounds and broken hearts."

JOHN HENDERSHOT, Christian Ministries

FAITH, HOPE, AND
Room for one more

One family's spiritual journey of shepherding
abused and handicapped children from around the world.

Jerry and Sandy Tucker

WITH LARRY AND CAROL TROXELL

Published by
GALILEAN HOME MINISTRIES PUBLISHING
Liberty, Kentucky 42539

FAITH, HOPE, AND ROOM FOR ONE MORE
BY JERRY AND SANDY TUCKER
WITH LARRY AND CAROL TROXELL

Copyright 1989 by Galilean Home Ministries, Inc.

Cover Photograph by Mark Kidd Studios of Kentucky

Printed in the United States of America

All rights reserved. No part of this book may be reproduced without permission from the publisher, except by a reviewer who may quote brief passages in a review; nor may any part of this book be reproduced, stored in a retrieval system or copied by mechanical, photocopying, recording or other means without permission from the publisher.

Jessica, 15, and Becky, 19

Dedication

This book is 27 years of love and dedication not only to the many children who have passed through our doors but to the dozens who will forever be in our care. We especially dedicate this book of memories and faith to Becky and Jessica who have shared their Mom and Dad unselfishly with hundreds of children. We give all honor and glory to the real Author of this book, Jesus Christ, who came into our lives through the leading of our children.

Take heed that ye despise not one of these little ones; for I say unto you, That in heaven their angels do always behold the face of my Father which is in heaven. Matt. 18:10

Thank you

We thank our staff for their dedication in helping care for the many children of the Galilean Home. They are: Lafern Blevins, Chris Burnett, Joy Calcina, Olivia Calcine, Hannah Callinan, Tim Callinan, Phyllis Chadwell, Charlotte Coffey, Crissy Cross, Teresa Denson, Phebe Dunlap, Susan Fowler, Drea Fowler, Faye Garrett, Angie Harris, Alice Lawless, Kathy Loveless, Tony Luce, Brenda Luce, Janet Luttrell, Alta Martin, Phyllis Matherly, Sammie Murphy, Angie Riggins, Sharon Roberts, Dorothy Salyers, Linda Singleton, Julie St. John, Paula Tague, Ila Tarter, Melody Taylor, Frank Tucker, Crissy Vaughn, Becky Wesley, Anita Wilson, Margaret Wimmer, Steven Wimmer, Ricky Wimmer, Doris Wooley, and Carolyn Zuercher.

The authors

Jerry and Sandy Tucker are the founders and directors of Galilean Home Ministries, a non-profit religious organization that ministers to abused and handicapped children. They reside at their Galilean Home on South Fork Ridge in Casey County, Kentucky with their two daughters, Rebecca and Jessica, and dozens of adopted and foster children from around the world. This book is told through Sandy's eyes because we felt it was best to write the story this way for the reader. However, this has been a joint venture by Jerry and Sandy, reflecting both their thoughts and convictions.

Larry and Carol Troxell are the founders and directors of Life Building Communications, a non-profit religious organization that assists ministries with their communication needs. They live in Somerset, Ky. and have one daughter, Flynn.

Jerry and Sandy on 25th wedding anniversary

PROLOGUE
A silver wedding anniversary
JANUARY, 1988

The Galilean Home Family, Fall 1987

7

An empty crib

The ear-piercing wail of a newborn baby broke the silent night not once, but twice. Two boys crying, reaching frantically for the touch of their mothers. The energetic waving of arms and legs, the wrinkled skin, the near bald heads, the all-knowing eyes taking in the face of the mother who has given them birth, whose face no longer mirrors the pain of labor but her boundless love for the son she now cuddles in her arms.

Thank You, Lord, for allowing me to deliver these two boys. As a midwife, I am always awed by the beauty of these moments as I deliver a child created in Your image. I rejoice for the mother and father who will never know the pain of being told they can't have a child as Jerry and I were.

After nearly seven years, Lord, You blessed us with an adopted son, Jeremy. Then You defied what the doctors said _ You presented us two precious girls of our own, Rebecca and

Jessica. And as a bonus Lord, You gave us all these unwanted children who need love, more than three dozen! We'll keep making room for them as long as You send them. Only You know the size of our hearts.

Rarely have I delivered two children this close together, but I don't mind. You kept Your end of the bargain, Lord. As our 25th wedding anniversary neared, it became evident our celebration and these two births would coincide, and I asked a very human request of You. Hold off delivery for these two women to allow Jerry and me this special time together. Such a beautiful anniversary it was, but the second we returned home, You put us back to work.

First, we were greeted by the children _ from Rosie barreling top speed through the house to give us a hug, to Weldon, the celebrity child, working his way through the crowd, lifting his little arms to be held.

Everyone tried to talk at once and exchange hugs and kisses. We learned Mam had fallen a few hours earlier, requiring 27 stitches in her forehead. That Mam. Now I know where Jerry, her grandson, gets his independence. Perhaps this 98-year-old great-grandmother will be convinced to let someone help her from bed to her wheel chair. I doubt it.

In the midst of the confusion, two calls came, Lord. Labor pains had begun for two young mothers. It was Your way of saying the party was over. But this was to be another first for the Galilean Home. Usually Margaret and I go to the mother's home for the delivery, but these babies won't wait _ their homes are nearly 70 miles apart. I had to ask both mothers to come here.

Everyone moved into action converting the Galilean Home into a birthing center. The small office next to my midwife clinic quickly became a birthing room. Jerry and the staff moved the desk out and a bed in just in time for our

Mennonite neighbor. Later, the family from near Lexington arrived and settled into the clinic.

I awoke Jerry before dawn.

"It's time. Put some hot water on."

He grabbed a robe and went running like a nervous, expectant father to the kitchen to boil a large kettle of water. He turned up the stereo to muffle the sounds of labor as not to disturb the sleeping children. Later, some of the children who were early to rise from the commotion wanted to know what was wrong. They rarely saw their bearded father in a robe and sandals.

Other children, noticing the large boiling pot on the stove, cried: "Oatmeal again?"

When they learned a mother was having a baby in our home, they became excited, their eyes beaming, and asking when "their baby" would arrive. Having new brothers and sisters join our family has become a way of life for them.

The Mennonite baby was born around 7 a.m., weighing more than 10 pounds! He joins two sisters at home. The second mother's labor lasted until the evening, with the staff and older children pacing the floor like expectant parents during the day. Around 9 p.m., the second mother gave birth, also a boy and the third child in his family.

What a blessing! As do many of Your blessings, Lord, my midwife practice came about in a strange way. When we were Mennonites, a need arose for a midwife in the community. I was elected _ I had witnessed a nurse deliver our oldest adopted girl's first child, and I had observed the delivery of a Mormon mother's baby one bleak winter night in our log cabin when we lived in Montana. As our family grew and we left the Mennonite order, I continued delivering babies _ these two today make 115 _ not only for our Mennonite neighbors but also for others like the family from near Lexington.

Lexington. Only a few hours ago we had been among the skyscrapers and concrete. Nothing like our ever-expanding log home nestled in the woods on South Fork Ridge in Casey County.

A supporter of our ministry had provided Jerry and I a penthouse suite in a Lexington luxury hotel for our anniversary. We had a private elevator that only went to our floor. The hotel suite was larger than our first apartment above a trailer park laundry when we married 25 years ago in Michigan.

Jerry surprised me with an anniversary dinner but not before he drove around town, stopping at different restaurants. Just as I would get ready to open the car door, he would say, "No, let's go some place else."

He continued this routine for what seemed hours. He was having fun at my expense as he stalled until our friends were assembled at a Japanese restaurant. I had expected Jerry to stage an out of the ordinary dinner but I never dreamed of such a special evening.

"Surprise!" everyone screamed as we entered the dining room. Some of our older children _ Jeremy, Becky, and Jessica _ were there, laughing at their mother, playing with chopsticks on the table, watching with awe as Oriental cooks performed antics with their knives. Several staff associates and friends were in the group. And my sister, Debbie and her family.

Debbie. Sisters married to brothers. Expecting with our first born at the same time. Wearing matching maternity clothes. Then mourning when her husband drowned. I thought of the years she and her three small children lived with us in Kentucky and Montana while Jerry and I were changing the spiritual direction of our lives, taking part for a season in the Mormon religion. Now here she was with us to celebrate 25

11

years together.

At the head of the table to lead in prayer was Frank, Jerry's dad. Dressed as he does every day _ jeans and shirt with a tie. How I cherish this man. He joined us to help care for our children when we returned to Kentucky. Running errands. Rocking babies to sleep. Whatever needs to be done, he's there for his dozens of "grandchildren." When he's not at our home, he opens his heart to visit the elderly at a nearby nursing home.

Don and Susan Fowler of Victory Ministries in Columbus, Ohio were there. I remembered all the times our cupboards were nearly bare and they came with truck loads of food for the children.

Then I spotted Mary Lou Weldy. She had gone with me to Haiti when You led us to bring surgically correctable children to America for treatment. I thought of the joy on Baby Marie's mother's face when we returned her daughter after successful surgery for water on the brain. All of our Haitian children _ Effie, Rose, Elenue, and Jean _ are continuing treatment. How precious they are to us.

Thank You, Lord, for the family, the friends and the memories from the dinner. Laughing with us as we related our fear of spending our evening trapped in our elevator only to discover the door could be unlocked with the key from our private suite. Our friends laughing hysterically at my bewilderment over a maid wanting to turn down our bed. I had never heard of such a hotel tradition _ I was fully capable of turning down my husband's bed! We got a kick out of Jerry wearing a red rose on his sweater, and watching him frequently slip away to call home to check on the other 24 children.

Family and friends were gathered around the tables, watching the chefs perform their art with steak, shrimp, and lobster _ food certainly not common at the Galilean Home.

Sandy and her sister Debbie, 1967

The dining room rang with voices and laughter as we all sampled the scrumptious meals. Even the storybook Japanese waitresses dressed in colorful kimonos, with satiny sashes that enhanced their tiny waists. The waitresses joined our fun while other restaurant guests stole curious glances at our group.

As the evening ended, we gathered in the main dining room for a photograph. What an unusual bunch we must have appeared. There were men in blue jeans, three-piece suits, ladies in slacks and also their Sunday best, and of course, the traditional Mennonite style of dress. All of us sharing hugs. Only one of us thought of bringing a camera, but no one wanted to be left out of the picture so we snatched a waitress passing by. She stopped everything to be our photographer.

She lifted the camera to her eye. "Mauve clos plez," she directed.

"Easier said than done," I thought. There were too many of us to fit in the picture. Three times she stepped back and tried to fit us all in the picture. She could move no further,

13

the shutter snapped, the flash flashed.

Possessions don't mean much to me but when I look at that picture, I relive that precious and blessed night.

The group followed us downtown, tooting their horns as if we were newlyweds. As Jerry and I trotted off for a romantic horse and carriage ride in the moonlight, Jerry called over his shoulder, "Don't forget to slop the hogs!"

Now we're back home with our children; but, Lord, an empty baby crib is outside our bedroom. You know it's empty but You know there's plenty of room for another child in our hearts.

That bed was to have been filled by Baby Alicia, our anniversary "gift." Jerry had returned dejected from a Louisiana hospital a few hours before our dinner without this three-week-old infant with club feet and spina bifida. Her unwed mother had asked if we would take her baby rather than allow the state to have the infant.

Lord, You know we have never been able to say no. The hospital declined to release her because she still needed a shunt implant. We will have to wait.

Waiting. We're used to it. Like the two years of red tape before Ernie and Robbie, two severely mentally retarded brothers from New York, were allowed to join our family. Or the hassle we've been undergoing for months to free Berto from a children's prison in Haiti. My heart aches when I think of the tears streaming down his face as I had to leave him behind when I left the orphanage.

In time, Lord, I know You will send Alicia to fill our empty crib, and Berto, and others. It was nearly seven years before You arranged for our first adopted son. Then, You used little children to lead us to You. Now You bring more and more to us.

What a journey it has been!

BOOK ONE
In search of children
1962-1974

Jerry and Sandy on their wedding day, Jan. 21, 1963

A day in the park

"Watch me!" Claudia squealed, gliding down the slide, her arms spread as if she were an airplane, the wind blowing her baby soft blonde hair against the clear blue skyline, all the time her giggling going full throttle.

Jerry and I laughed as she crashed into the sand, abruptly landing on her knees. She pulled herself up, racing back to do it again. Claudia's older brother noticed the fun and decided to interrupt.

As she climbed the steps, he walked up the slide, holding onto the edges. They met at the top with him laughing, "Beat you," and Claudia yelling, "No fair!" But Claudia's anger turned back to laughter as she played fighter pilot, chasing her brother in hot pursuit down the slide.

"Look, Jerry, Cory is going to try the slide." The towheaded toddler had been playing with his dump truck in the nearby sandbox when Claudia's squeals had captured his attention. His brown eyes were as big as saucers in amazement, a grin crossing his angel face.

He had decided to brave the slide himself. Before I could move, Claudia had seen him.

"No! You're too little," she said to Cory, taking his hand. "Come on, I'll help you swing."

"Claudia's got mothering instincts already built in," I said.

"Yes, she's a beautiful child," Jerry answered.

An older boy noticed Claudia helping Cory try to swing. He went to the adjoining swing, and started to see how high he could go.

"Jason, stop it! He can't swing with you going that high. You're scaring him," Claudia yelled.

"Someone needs to take a switch to that boy," I fumed.

"I bet he doesn't have a father at home," Jerry replied. "It's obvious he's not had any discipline."

Jason finally stopped his harassing, having spotted some other boys with a basketball. Cory clinched the swing chains with his tiny fists, laughing as Claudia gently pushed him.

The park's kiddie section was brimming with small children. Older ones were on the larger rides like the roller coaster and it appeared the younger children had been left here.

Jerry and I were lost in the giggles, the screams of delight, even the antics of the children who were fussy.

"Way to go!" Jerry and I almost yelled simultaneously, clapping at Cory's victory. He was now swinging by himself with little Claudia maintaining a close eye, ready to reach out and catch him if he were to fall.

"They're such beautiful children," I heard someone beside me side say.

17

"Yes, they are," I responded nervously.

"What are their names?" she asked, nodding to Claudia and Cory.

I suddenly felt trapped. What do I say?

"I don't know."

"But aren't those two children on the swings yours?"

"No."

Jerry took my arm as I stood up from the bench. "I guess it's time we left," he said.

As I looked back over my shoulder for a final glimpse of Claudia and Cory, or whatever their names were, I saw the woman staring at me with a puzzled look on her face as if I were crazy.

Didn't this woman with her accusing eyes know what it was like to be unable to bear children? Couldn't she understand how hard we had tried to adopt? Couldn't she see our coming to the park was a way to be close to children, to ease the pain we had carried for more than six years of marriage?

Jerry and I often went to the park. We would sit for hours absorbing the children playing, the sound of their laughter. We would pick our favorites and give them names, like Claudia and Cory today. Children who enjoyed life but kept an eye out for others like little Claudia giving smaller Cory a hand.

We would even select children we thought had a discipline problem and talk about how we would shape them up with love. It amazed us how many parents just dropped their children at the park alone or sent them with older brothers and sisters. Didn't they realize what they were missing by failing to be with them? Children grow up so fast _ the time not spent with them could never be replaced.

Within a month after Jerry and I were married, I visited

18

a physician.

"Mrs. Tucker, I think you're jumping to conclusions too fast," he laughed. He told me that I was not expecting a baby yet, and to come back in six months.

Jerry and I began to plan for a baby. As quickly as we could, we found a house in a new subdivision in Livonia. After we eloped, we had rented an apartment above the Wagon Wheel Trailer Park Laundry in Farmington, Michigan. But our baby wasn't going to grow up over any laundry!

Our first house project was to decorate the baby's room.

Her nursery _ naturally, I knew our first baby would be a girl _ had to be picture perfect, all frills. We installed soft, plush pink carpet on the floor so our baby wouldn't scuff her tiny hands and knees. And I picked out pink, flowery wallpaper with streamers of silk ribbons among the blossoms and, of course, I hung lacy curtains. I loved how the sunlight danced through the lace, leaving delicate shadows around the room.

Jerry came home one day with a dressing table he had purchased for his baby girl to be. The doors were green with Pennsyslvania Dutch trim and I happily stocked it with diapers and gowns. The fragrance of baby powder filled the room. The final triumph was a canopy covered crib, trimmed in pink and white eyelet and ribbons. This room was perfect for the beautiful baby girl we were certain would soon sleep in that crib.

Six months later I had not conceived. Six months turned into six years and still no baby. Sometimes the pain would become too heavy to bear and I would slip into the silent nursery and gently rock the empty and waiting cradle, certain that somehow, someway, the cradle would not remain empty forever.

Heaven knows Jerry and I tried. We went for fertility

tests at Henry Ford Hospital in Detroit. I underwent explora-
tory surgery. I was willing to try anything the doctors could
think of that would help me have a baby.

But nothing worked.

Jerry's fertility had been damaged from mumps as a
child. We underwent extensive testing to determine our chance
of conceiving. Finally, we heard the results.

"You have only a million to one chance of ever having
your own children," the doctor said.

Our hearts were broken. It was like saying we had no
chance at all.

We applied to adoption agencies and struck out there
too. One excuse after another. We had to be married for three
years to even apply. We were too young _ I was 18, Jerry 22.
They even said we were too immature.

Since I was Catholic, we went to Catholic Charities
and applied for adoption. We thought we deserved a perfect
baby _ a blonde haired girl with blue eyes under two years old.
However, we were willing to consider any child.

It wasn't to be. They said we didn't attend church
enough.

"How do you know how often we attend?" I asked in
disbelief, knowing we faithfully attended church.

"By the envelopes," the priest said in a written state-
ment to the social worker handling our application. A record
of our gifts was kept from the tithing envelopes. But we didn't
always use the envelopes for our offering.

We were rejected because we allegedly were too
young, too immature, and didn't regularly attend church.

Still, we wouldn't give up. I went back for more
fertility studies. I tried artificial insemination about half a
dozen times, at $25 a session. Nothing happened.

To my horror and embarrassment, I eventually discovered medical interns were donors for the artificial insemination. The $25 application fee was to provide them with extra money for medical school! This was the final, worst embarrassment. As if suffering through all the testing weren't enough, now it seemed the whole world knew. These people were making a profit from our grief.

As each month went by, the disappointment deepened. The doctors said I wanted to conceive so desperately that my body chemistry fought it.

Jerry and I decided that if we couldn't have children or adopt, then we had to be as close to them as possible. We spent hours spent at the park, or baby-sitting for my neighbors, or teaching catechism classes at the church, or volunteering at a Catholic orphanage.

When an attempt to adopt a child would fall through, I would throw myself into volunteer work.

Once I volunteered at Wayne County State Hospital. One day when I was working in the suicide ward, I discovered a young woman by the telephone in the hallway, a suitcase by her feet.

"Going somewhere?" I asked.

A smile broke across her face. "Yes, today I'm going home to my children." She pulled a photo album from her purse and proceeded to proudly show me pictures of her three small children.

"They're so pretty. She's going home today," I said, turning to a nurse walking by.

"No, Sandy. She does this routine every day."

Stunned, I turned back to face the young mother. She looked me in the eye, threw her head back and started laughing. She picked up her suitcase and went down the hall, continuing to laugh insanely.

Tears welled up in my eyes. That experience hurt so

deeply I never returned. I decided that any more volunteer work would be directly with children. I couldn't erase the picture of those three children from my mind as if they were asking "Where's Mommy?"

I switched to sharing my time at the Sarah Fisher Home, a Catholic orphanage. I was assigned to Jennifer, a 7-year-old who had been neglected by her parents. Three times a week I visited and we would do all kinds of things together, including spending a day at the Sarah Fisher Campgrounds. Jennifer would cling to me as I would struggle to help her with her bathing suit _ she loved to swim but she always insisted I stay by her side.

I wanted to adopt Jennifer even though I had been told in the beginning her parents still retained legal custody. When I saw that my fantasy would not become reality, I quit going _ the pain was more than I could bear. Sometimes I cried to God wondering where He was.

I also returned to my church to teach classes on the Catholic religion. My interest was not so much in teaching as it was in being with the children.

Our neighbors frequently let us baby-sit. The pink lacy nursery was now filled with a variety of children but none of them mine. God knew that if I couldn't have my own, I'd gather others and be with as many children as I could. I ached and longed for one of my own. Nobody knew how my heart throbbed when I saw a newborn baby. It instantly became mine!

I was a part-time mother caring for other women's children. It certainly was not what I had expected when Jerry and I married six years ago.

A stormy beginning

"Sandy, Larry's got this friend. Come on, let's go on a double date," Betty pleaded as we rushed between orders for burgers and fries at the A&W Root Beer Stand.

"Don't have time for that stuff. I'll be here until 2 in the morning and then I have to be at school by 8," I said, swiping a lock of my newly bleached blonde hair out of my face as I headed for the next car.

Betty wouldn't let up.

"Come on, Sandy. An old school buddy of Larry's just got out of the Army," Betty said. "It will be fun, the four of us going out together."

"What's his name?"

"Jerry Tucker."

"I've heard of him. Isn't he divorced?"

"Yeah, but he's a real nice guy, Sandy."

"There's no way my parents would let their good

Catholic girl go out with a divorced man."

Betty persisted. She hounded me when we passed between the cars and again as we piled hamburgers onto our trays. Every chance she got. And when Larry showed up later, there was Jerry standing tall and military straight and looking real tan in the night lights. I heard myself saying "Yes" and I prayed my parents didn't find out who he was.

The four of us went to a drive-in movie. Instead of watching the film, Jerry and I spent the time talking. I learned he had gotten out of the Army about six months earlier and returned to laying concrete blocks for Al Ferguson who he had worked for while in high school.

That first evening was fun but all the time I knew there would be trouble. My parents would never accept a divorced man.

A short time later, Jerry turned 22. I was almost 18, just out of high school and learning to be a beautician.

Shortly after we began dating, I quit the car hopping job and went to work at Cunningham's Drug Store as a waitress at their lunch counter. Cunningham's was a hangout for local teen-agers. All green vinyl and brightly polished chrome under fluorescent lights. When evening came, teens would fill the booths drinking sodas and eating hamburgers. The place buzzed with the sound of young voices.

As soon as he cleaned up from work, here would come Jerry, slipping onto one of the green vinyl counter stools. He became Cunningham's best customer as he waited patiently for me to finish work. In between customers, we made small talk as I polished Coke rings from the counter top.

If the boss gave him a "you're holding the stool too long" look, Jerry would order another Coke. As a teen-age girl, I thought he looked so cool in his jeans and T-shirt with his crisp Army manners. Tanned muscles showed from under the rolled up shirt sleeves. I was the envy of all my girl friends!

Then one evening he was unusually quiet, his thoughts apparently somewhere else. Our usual easy chatter was strained _ was I about to be dumped, let down easy? Finally, the restaurant closed for the evening and we walked out into the darkness.

"I've got a confession," Jerry said.

Weird ideas raced through my mind. Was he on the run from the law? Was there another girl? What was this big confession?

"Sandy, I'm not divorced."

Oh, no, my mother is going to kill me, I thought. I've been dating a married man! I was so stunned. I didn't know what to say so I just waited. But Jerry had another shocker for me.

For what seemed an eternity, Jerry was silent in the darkness. Finally, "The truth is, I've never been married."

"But you're divorced. Everybody says so. Even your father told me you were divorced." I had become good friends with Jerry's dad, Frank, who worked in Jerry's construction crew. He was separated from Jerry's mother, Catherine.

"I know what my dad said, but it's not true."

Jerry explained that when he was 19 he ran away with a 16-year-old Indian girl. They went to South Carolina where she could get married without parental approval. The problem was she had forgotten her birth certificate and no justice of the peace would marry them.

"We ran away to get married and so the only thing to do was to come back married."

Jerry said they went to Birmingham, Alabama where his mother's folks were from. They moved in with his aunt and lived as though they were married.

"I worked in a paper mill for awhile but after a few

25

months we began to feel uncomfortable at my aunt's.

"We decided to come back to Michigan. Anyway when we came back to Detroit, her parents, my parents, my grandparents, everybody thought we were married. Nobody asked to see a marriage license. We rented an apartment and I went back to work for Al.

"Our plan was to let everyone think we were married and when she turned 18, we were going to slip down to the courthouse and make it official."

But the masquerade didn't last. That winter, work became scarce and Jerry joined the Army.

"Our relationship just fell apart. We let everybody think we divorced _ even my parents. I haven't told anybody different."

I grieved for how Jerry had been hurt, but learning he hadn't been married was a relief. What complaint could my parents have now?

"Sandy, when I came out of the Army last spring, I led a pretty wild life. Honkytonking every night. Al had to bail me out of jail a couple of times. Wild parties. Cruising around. I was just a 21-year-old guy impressing the girls with my big money and this big tattoo on my arm." Jerry's tattoo was of a dagger sticking through the head of a panther with the inscription "Born To Raise Hell."

I didn't necessarily like the Jerry I was hearing about. I sensed, however, he was pouring out his soul to me.

"Sandy, the night before I met you that first time, I was partying at a bar. But when I met you, it was BANG! Over night you pulled the reins in on me. No more wild partying. Sandy, this hasn't been a gradual thing for me. I was crazy about you after that first date.

"You know where I am after work now. I'm at Cunningham's waiting for you."

26

Jerry had always seemed like the "good boy next door" with his polite manners and clean language. My heart pounded as he confessed the truth about his past and his feelings for me.

We talked for a long time that night as he held my hand. I knew I was being drawn to this man. Was he going to ask me to marry him?

"I'm going deer hunting with Al for a couple of weeks up in northern Michigan. When I get back we'll talk more." What a letdown _ after all this, he was going hunting with Al. I spent a restless night wondering what lay ahead.

The next morning I heard a truck pull up in front of my house. From the doorway I saw Jerry coming up the sidewalk dressed in his hunting clothes. On the street was the old junk truck that Jerry and his boss had rigged up for their numerous hunting and fishing trips. They had built a frame to support a tent on the truck bed. I saw his boss in the truck as I opened the door. I couldn't help laughing at these grown men going out to play hunters.

Jerry's long legs took the front walk in quick strides as he bounded up to the door.

"Will you marry me?"

Stunned and without hesitation, I said, "Yes."

He handed me a ring. "I love you. I'll see you when I get back from deer hunting. Got to go."

"I love you, too," I said, looking at my ring, and waving as he ran back to the truck.

Ten days later, he returned nearly frozen to death and without having killed any deer. During their 200-mile trip, water from the highway had splashed on the tent, covering it in a sheet of ice, leaving them an igloo to sleep in for nearly two weeks. But it was the separation from me that had really made his life miserable, Jerry said. I discovered he had bought my engagement ring just before stopping at my house on his way deer hunting.

At first, my mother was thrilled about my engagement. However, when she learned Jerry was Protestant and heard the rumors he was divorced, she hit the ceiling. She refused to believe Jerry's story about his past, no matter how hard I pleaded that it was the truth.

Mildred Burda, born to Polish immigrants, would loudly warn me that I was crazy to believe this non-Catholic. Her boisterous conversation never stopped from the moment she arrived home from work at J.L. Hudson's Department Store through dinner, almost always yelling how I was making the biggest mistake of my life. My father, also Polish, would listen to my mother and quietly nod when my mother would say, "Isn't that right, Gene?"

I secretly believed she ranted so because she would be losing her babysitter. Being the oldest, I had always helped her with my slightly retarded brother Pat, my sister Debbie, and Perry, my youngest brother.

Debbie, 11, and Perry, 9, formed what Debbie called the "Jerry Haters Club." They heard my mother's constant badgering about destroying my life, and decided they didn't like Jerry either. He was always teasing Debbie, doing anything to aggravate her. He nicknamed Perry "Ma Ma's Little Boy" since he was the baby of the family and spoiled.

When I would cook for Jerry, they both would fold their arms at the table and say that the "Jerry Haters Club" didn't believe in eating with him. Once, when I had spent hours preparing a meat loaf for Jerry, Debbie hid it inside the back of the television. We searched forever looking for the food and it was hours before Debbie confessed where she had hidden it.

Jerry and I had not set a wedding date, but here I was

an engaged woman and my mother started treating me like a child. My curfew went from 11 to 10 then to 9 o'clock. She checked my clothing, searched my room, accused me of sleeping with Jerry. That hurt deeply. I had always believed in saving myself for my husband.

One day after a heated disagreement with my mother, I stormed out of the house, crying over her lack of trust in me. We were adults and in love. Why couldn't she understand? I walked and cried for hours, paying no attention to where I was going. Soon it was dark and I realized I must have traveled a good 10 miles.

Now I was really frightened. I was too upset and hurt to call my parents. If I called Jerry and he took me home, that would only add fuel to the fire. I called Jerry's boss, Al, and he and his wife Pat came for me.

Jerry met me at Al's. We decided to end the arguments with my parents and elope. Like every young girl, I had always dreamed of a church wedding and walking down the aisle in a white wedding dress; but being with Jerry was more important. We were in love. I stayed with Pat and Al until we could arrange the wedding.

Soon after, we found an apartment over the laundry room at Wagon Wheel Trailer Park and located furniture to start housekeeping. Then with Al and Pat as witnesses, we were married before a justice of the peace in Redford, Michigan near their home. The four of us drove down to Toledo, Ohio to have a honeymoon dinner at a Howard Johnson's Restaurant.

It was January 21, 1963. Jerry and I had only known each other for about four months but I knew I wanted to spend the rest of my life with this man and to be the best wife in the world.

As for my parents, their hearts were broken over our

eloping. They had eloped too _ and had wanted a church wedding for their daughter. As the months progressed, and Jerry and I began trying to have children, my parents still refused to talk to me.

Once when my mother spotted me in K mart, she grabbed Debbie by the arm and ushered her out without speaking. When I would telephone, Debbie would usually answer and hang up at Mother's directions. As much as I loved Jerry, I felt a deep sense of loss at my parents' rejection. I longed for a reconciliation. I wanted them to know how happy Jerry and I were.

We had begun attending the Catholic Church near our apartment. Jerry, who had attended the Church of Christ as a child, took classes and joined the Catholic Church for me. The priest arranged for a church wedding _ I could wear the white wedding gown I had always dreamed of, but I had to leave the veil off my face since I was already married.

Yielding to a last minute plea, my parents agreed to attend the wedding after they learned Jerry had joined the Catholic Church. They saw their daughter in a church ceremony eight months to the day from when Jerry and I eloped. It was also Jerry's Grandmother Mam's birthday. My father tearfully walked me down the aisle and gave me away with his blessing.

Our biggest dream was to have a child. The months passed into years and still no children. I had to be content with watching children in the park and being a part-time mother as I baby-sat for my neighbors' children.

One day, Jerry came home, excitedly running through the house, calling for me. As usual, I was in the nursery, trying to coax a neighbors' child to take a nap.

"Don't yell so loud," I whispered as I closed the nursery door. "You'll wake him up."

I noticed Jerry had tears forming around his eyes as he slipped his arm around me in the hallway.

As we walked back to the living room, I asked, "Honey, what's wrong?"

"Al knows this girl ..."

"Yeah, what about her?"

"This teen-age girl has a baby ..."

"Really ..."

"Yeah, a baby boy ... he's got some kind of problem ... and they had to operate ... he's got these plastic tubes coming out of his nose ..."

"Poor little thing. Is he going to be all right?"

"Sure, but, Honey, you don't understand. The mother doesn't want him!"

"What?"

"She's just a child herself and the baby needs medical attention. Sandy, she doesn't want her baby ..."

"Honey, are you thinking what I'm thinking?"

"Al says she'll let someone have the baby if they'll pay off the medical bills. Sweetheart, Al wants to know if we want the baby?"

"I've got a son!"

My feet are numb from pacing the floor and with almost every pass across the room, I stumble over this stupid polar bear rug. Jerry's precious rug!

Al says we'll need $500 for the medical and legal fees plus $50 a week for the foster mother until the adoption is finalized.

$500! Jerry's making good money but it seems to slip away from us. You would have thought we would have learned from our bankruptcy to save money for a rainy day. Now the rainy day is here and no money. I've trimmed the grocery bill as much as I can but still there's the mortgage payment and the new car and, of course, the furniture.

Maybe one of those consolidation loans would trim the payments. It's certain there's nothing left to trim out of the budget. I've cut it to the bone and we still aren't even close to $500. Every time I think of the money we've blown over the years I could cry. What do I mean "could cry" _ I am crying! All those trips to Niagara Falls. The money from one of thosewould be more than enough. Niagara Falls and this stupid bear skin rug _ we paid $800 for this thing!

"Honey!"

"Jerry, did you call me?"

"Yeah, Al's here!"

"Oh, great. Just when I don't need company."

" _ and I think he has the baby!"

Troubles forgotten, my heart is in my throat, my ears are pounding and my knees are like putty. Al's big car is in the driveway. He's coming toward the house. Al _ over six feet tall _ is wearing a beaming grin on his weathered face. He is carrying a tiny bundle of white in those strong arms.

"Sandy, aren't you going to open the door?" Al laughs and slowly pulls back the blanket. Just like the glass windows of a hospital nursery, the window in my storm door is all that separates mc from my baby. Yes, my baby, my son!

For most women, that first moment with their baby comes at birth in a hospital delivery room surrounded by doctors and nurses in their sterile white surgical clothes. For me, it came in our living room with Al _ looking like Dean Martin in his dress jeans and white shirt _ placing this 17 pound, scrawny three-and-a-half-month-old boy in my arms.

I sat on the couch and laid him carefully in my lap. I had held lots of babies before but this one was different _ he was going to be ours!

Jerry and I couldn't wait to see this miracle God had sent us. I carefully pulled the baby shawl away so we could get our first look at each other. Al said the child's name was Curt but we had decided to rename him Jeremy.

Jeremy was a long baby, pale and underweight. His head rested on my knees and his arms stretched in all directions. His head, crowned with light brown hair, twisted and turned this way and that way as his large dark eyes took in new faces. Two chocolate drop eyes, huge in his small face, met mine and stared at me as if we shared the most wonderful secrets. I carefully examined two delicate ears and counted 10 tiny toes and 10 tiny fingers.

Those tiny fingers tightly grasped one of Jerry's and held on for dear life. Jerry laughed and giggled while I cried. Even with those green tubes in his nose from the surgery, Jeremy was beautiful. A beautiful, perfect baby and he was going to be ours!

All too soon Al loaded Jeremy into the car and was gone. I was in an euphoric daze. Friends had told me about that moment right after birth. The doctor lays the baby in the mother's arms and the pain of childbirth is suddenly forgotten. It is replaced with a sweet wonderful mixture of mother's love and exhaustion.

What a wonderful feeling! I had heard some mothers cried when their babies were born. It had sounded really strange at the time _ why in the world cry when they had been so wonderfully blessed? Suddenly, it didn't sound odd.

As the car disappeared down the street, I walked back into the house, closing the door as the tears flowed. As I thought of the $500 we needed, the remembrance of our past bankruptcy came crashing over me. I felt an unseen force rise in my stomach as if it were going to reach up and choke me. Would I be denied the child I had waited for all these years.

I remembered sitting in a Florida motel room waiting for word from Jerry. Our vacation had been interrupted by a phone call from one of our employees at J and S Tucker Construction. We were told the Internal Revenue Service had seized our bank account and the employees' payroll checks were bouncing all over Michigan.

Sandy with Jeremy on second visit to foster mother's.

A couple of years after we were married, Jerry had decided to go into business for himself. Why give all this profit to Al? After all, it was Jerry who nearly ran the business for him. Why not run one for ourselves?

We grew to 40 employees almost overnight, including the 18 Jerry took with him from Al's Allstate Trenching _ most of them friends and family members. My Aunt Elaine quit her job at Ford Motor Company to become our secretary, and my father left the City of Detroit transportation department to work as our mechanic. If someone needed a job, we gave it to them. After all, the money was rolling in. Before we discovered we didn't know a hill of beans about business however, it was too late. When the economy faltered, there was not enough money to meet our exorbitant payroll and to make payments on all the top-of-the-line equipment we had purchased. We had $50,000 in accounts payable but we couldn't collect because the IRS had frozen them.

After we lost our business, Jerry worked alone for

awhile and then approached Al, who had always been like an older brother to him, about giving him a job. He did, but Jerry had to start back as a block layer. To keep from losing our house, they worked out a deal for Al to buy it for $1 and assume our mortgage, then rent it back to us.

It's been three years since we filed bankruptcy. Yet even now I'm choking from the memories of all those months of stress, all those months of trying to come up with tens of thousands of dollars to save our business. All we need at the moment is $500, but it might as well be a million.

Where was the $500 to come from? My feet stumbled over the polar bear rug _ again. I took out my frustration on the rug, giving it a swift kick. Then with tears dripping from my chin, my sobbing and sniffing stopped and a grin crept over my face. An idea was forming in my mind. If we had been dumb enough to pay $800 for that rug, surely someone else would do the same.

My Jerry, he's so calm it's frustrating. The money doesn't seem to bother him at all. There goes Jerry across the yard to brag to the neighbors about "his" boy while I'm in here going crazy. I could scream!

I began cutting the food budget to save the extra $50 a week for the foster mother. We could eat beans and more beans. Even Tom could cut back.

Tom is Jerry's youngest brother who came to live with us while he finishes high school. Their mother's sudden death last spring stunned the family and Jerry insisted on taking in Tom. We bought him his first car _ a 1958 Buick _ for $50, and I taught him how to drive. Was that an experience!

No matter how hard I tried to save money, it ended up costing us more than the $50 we paid the foster mother. There were diapers and other baby necessities. Gas for the car for the hour-long drives to the foster mother's. And of course all the little gifts I took Jeremy each visit.

But each time I saw Jeremy I knew somehow we would make it. Just to be able to hold him, kiss his tiny face, to gently suction out the green tubes in his nose, to change his diaper _ it all meant so much to me. I would do anything to make sure Jeremy became ours.

I knew Jerry was concerned about the $500 we would need to pay for the costs of the adoption and hospital medical expenses. We were struggling just to come up with the extra weekly expenses and simply were not making any progress in saving. But Jerry didn't allow his concern to show.

When we were together with our neighbors Vince and Nancy Candela and Bob and Nancy Carlson, all Jerry could talk about was adopting Jeremy. The dream of a child of our own was about to come true after all these years.

We had many fun times together, but mostly we talked about children. Nancy Carlson and I baby-sat for the Candelas' oldest son, Vincie, and when Nancy became pregnant with their second child, Dino, I was with her throughout her pregnancy. Within the last year, we rejoiced as the Carlsons successfully adopted their first son, Stephen.

Jerry and I never stopped dreaming. Time and again Jerry said, "If we're ever able to adopt a child, I'm going to climb to the top of this house and shout it from the rooftop."

About a month later, we heard from Al.

"Guess what? The judge says the adoption will be completed within the next week. Meet me at the courthouse and bring the money. You're going to get your baby."

The reality of Jeremy becoming ours struck like a thunderbolt. I had not expected it so soon. Reality was that time had run out. We were so close to having Jeremy but we didn't have the money. So close but so far _ the greatest disappointment of my life was about to come crashing over me when my eyes fell on the polar bear rug. We would have the $500 and our baby!

"Have a good day, Jerry. See you tonight."

Before Jerry even made it out of the driveway, I began folding the polar bear rug. First, I folded in the head, scratching my hand on the big teeth protruding from the open jaw, then each of the legs. I then rolled it into a big ball. I was starting to take short, sharp breaths from the weight and was so excited that I dropped it when I first picked it up. One of our four white poodles, Mimi, who had chewed off some of the bear's claws, started yelping and nipping at my heels as I made my way to the door, heaving the rug with every step.

This thing must weigh a ton! It's nine feet long and I'm only 5 foot 5 and 120 pounds. The door slammed back in my face before I could get the rug out the doorway.

"What are you doing?" yelled one of my neighbors as I began to stuff the rug into the trunk of our Thunderbird. I just waved and giggled to myself _ if I were unable to sell it, I wanted to be back home before Jerry so he wouldn't know that I had taken it out of the house!

To my surprise, no one really jumped at the polar bear rug. Oh sure, they liked it, but either they wouldn't give me $800 for it or they wanted to sell it on consignment.

I went from furniture stores to flea markets to craft shops. The unbelievable thing was, I had to tote that huge piece of dead weight out of the car into the store and unroll it for the owner at each stop. And when we couldn't work out a deal, I would refold it and sling it back over my shoulder and drag it back to the car again. Then I would have to stuff it back into the trunk. I couldn't help but think it must have been like a gangster stuffing a dead body into a trunk.

We hadn't been to church in awhile but I found myself praying as the afternoon wore on and my desperation increased. "God, I need to sell this rug to get my baby. You've got to help me."

My last stop was a furniture store in Plymouth, Michigan, about 10 miles from our home.

"I think I can get $700 for it. That's real quality even if your dog did chew off some of the claws," the dealer said. My heart gave a leap! "You leave it with me and let me see what I can do."

My heart fell. I finally had someone who wanted the rug but he too wanted to sell it on consignment. Didn't anyone understand I couldn't take Jeremy on consignment while I waited for this stupid rug to sell?

"But I need the money today. Cash."

"Fine, but the best I can do is $500."

I could have shouted but managed to keep my composure as we closed the deal. If that dealer only knew what I was going to use that money for! People in cars on the freeway must have thought I was crazy. All alone in the car and laughing to myself. I was on top of the world. By the time I arrived home, Jerry's truck was in the driveway.

"Sandy, where's the polar bear rug?"

I held up five $100 bills in front of him.

"Jerry, we have our baby!"

The $500 was paid and we were on our way home. I wasn't on Cloud 9 that late September day in 1969 _ it was at least Cloud 999! For five consecutive weeks, we had visited Jeremy at the foster mother's but now the adoption was final and Jeremy was officially ours. We were going home a family!

Jeremy was wearing his new outfit _ blue pants, blue

shirt, blue booties, blue sweater _ everything was blue, blue, blue. He would have to sleep in the pink bedroom with the lacy curtains I had always planned for a baby girl but he was dressed fit for a king!

"Sandy, all the neighbors are in the front yard."

I began to laugh. "Honey, look at the sign on the house."

As I got out of the car, the women started moving toward me, wanting to see the baby.

Across the full length of our house was a handmade banner with "Climb and Shout!" in huge bold letters. And Tom was standing by a ladder at the corner of the house.

I saw my handsome husband, Mr. Cool who never got excited, take off in a dead run like an Olympic sprinter. His neighborhood buddies began cheering as Jerry ran up the ladder, two and three steps at a time, to the top of the roof, and then lift his arms and shout, his joy echoing from the rooftops of the neighborhood.

"I'VE GOT A SON!"

A million to one miracle

"Sandy, watch Jeremy dive."

My head hurt as I struggled to look up. Jeremy was diving into the swimming pool for the hundredth time that summer day. We had bought one of those new above ground pools. Since we didn't have enough room for it in our back yard, my parents had insisted we install it in theirs.

After all, this was the practical thing to do. Practical? Definitely. It also meant they could spend most afternoons with their grandson.

Jeremy was nearly a year old. The green tubes in his nose were gone and he had gained weight _ he was now a healthy 35 pounds. The three of us went everywhere together _ restaurants, the zoo, the park where we had watched little Cory play years ago. But swimming was Jeremy's favorite pastime.

"Look, Sandy, my grandson is having the time of his

life," my mother laughed, beaming with pride. "He's making the biggest waves I've ever seen."

"Yes, Mom, but I don't feel too well today." I was thrilled my parents had fallen in love with Jeremy. He was their only grandchild and the center of their lives. They were so happy for Jerry and I _ the hard feelings before our marriage had been erased by this chubby dolphin playing in the pool.

Even the pain our bankruptcy had created wasn't held against us. My father had suffered a nervous breakdown when our business folded. The City of Detroit gave him a job back, despite his inner ear problems, but he lost a large chunk of his seniority which cut deeply into his pocketbook. We had become a big happy family, thanks in part to this grandson splashing in the pool. Adding to the excitement surging through the family was my sister Debbie. She had recently married Jerry's younger brother Michael, and was now expecting. Jerry's brother Richard and his wife Linda, had just become the proud parents of a baby girl, Jennifer.

The next morning I felt even worse. The vomiting had continued for days and the headaches _ these were worse than the migraines I had as a child. Especially on Mondays when I had to stay for Catechism classes. What on earth was wrong? Maybe a brain tumor. Was I was dying?

I had never felt so bad in all my life. After all these years of waiting for Jeremy, why was God dealing me this cruel blow?

"Debbie, can you watch Jeremy for me today? I've got to see a doctor. The vomiting won't stop and my head is pounding. I feel like I'm dying."

"Sure, Sandy. Just drop Jeremy off on the way to the doctor's office."

I hated bothering Debbie but I had to do something about this pain.

42

The doctor ran some tests and came back into the examining room, wearing a grim face.

"Mrs. Tucker, I'm afraid you have something that can't be cured."

I sat up on the edge of the examining table, clutching the sheet to me. Questions flashed through my mind.

"What was it? A brain tumor? I was right! Why God? Why take me away from Jerry and Jeremy?"

Noticing the apparent fear on my face, the doctor said, "Settle down, Mrs. Tucker. No need to be frightened. True, it can't be cured but the problem will take care of itself."

Now I was really confused. Cure itself?

"What are you trying to tell me doctor?"

A grin spread across his face. "You're going to have a baby."

"A BABY!" I shouted. I was so shocked I jumped up, the sheet falling to the floor. I jumped back on the table, clutching the sheet to me, laughing and crying at the same time.

"Mrs. Tucker, you've just been experiencing morning sickness. I would say you're two to three months along."

Somehow I managed to get the Thunderbird back to Debbie's in one piece. I forgot I was even sick. I forgot the pain, the nausea! My mind was flooded with the wonderful knowledge that there was a tiny human life growing inside me.

A "one in a million chance."

"Guess what?" I asked Debbie, laughing and dancing up and down.

"Sandy, what in the world is going on?"

I shouted, "I'm going to have a baby!" and took my son from my sister's arms and playfully tossed him into the air.

"Jeremy, you're going to have a baby brother or

sister!" Debbie stood there in shock. Was this for real? There had been so many false alarms before. She grabbed me in a bear hug and the three of us danced around the living room.

Since Debbie's husband worked with Jerry, I stayed at her house, knowing Jerry had to bring Michael home. His truck pulled into the driveway and I ran out to meet him.

"Honey, guess what?" I ran up and hugged him, beaming from ear to ear. "I went to the doctor's office today just like you told me."

The expression on his face was total confusion. He had left me deathly ill earlier in the day and now here I was smiling, my eyes dancing with mischievous glee.

Watching his face, I laughed, "We're going to have a baby."

"Oh yeah, and I'm Tiny Tim," he responded, not reacting positively. He had heard news like this before, only to have his hopes shattered later.

"Aren't you excited?"

My happiness apparently was contagious. This was for real! Finally, realizing this was not a cruel joke, Jerry's face lit up. He hugged me, lifted me off my feet, and began spinning us both in a circle as we both laughed and cried joyously.

The following months were lived in a daze. I was so giddy with joy I just floated through life. Everything was perfect. Nothing could go wrong.

"Jeremy, you're going to have a baby sister real soon," I would say to him as I did the laundry. No doubt about it, this was a girl. "Million to one chance the doctors told me, but Jeremy, we won the jackpot. We're going to have a baby."

Since Debbie was already going to have a baby, we bought matching maternity clothes. We did everything in doubles. My mother even threw us a double baby shower.

44

When she learned I was truly going to have a baby, she danced a jig around the living room. Her two daughters were going to give her two more grandchildren. It was going to be great.

The months flew by and finally early one frosty November morning, my water broke. I called for Jerry at work and the secretary reached him on his truck phone. He was there in minutes, reassuring me that everything would be fine.

The doctors induced labor but it was 20 more hours before our daughter was born. I was in so much pain I cried and the doctor yelled at me for creating such a ruckus. Jerry became angry with the doctor for treating me with such unkindness.

I could not believe the way I was being treated. This wasn't the way it was supposed to be. Where was the joy? Where was the love? Giving birth should be the ultimate expression of love. I had waited years for this moment. Jerry was the only one trying to help me as he rubbed my back, attempting to ease the pain, and kissed away my tears.

Somehow through the pain I could hear Jerry talking to me. "Now, Grin, (that was his nickname for me when I would talk about children), if you can hold on until after midnight, the baby will be born on your birthday."

"If it were five minutes before midnight right now, I wouldn't want to wait," I cried. The doctors said the baby was coming in a posterior position with our backbones rubbing against each other. It felt like a concrete truck was racing over my back. Eventually they gave me a spinal.

Finally, thank heavens, the pain ended. I was so tired, _ all I wanted to do was sleep. Minutes later, the doctor placed my daughter in my arms. This miracle _ a tiny baby, six and a half pounds, looking like a little bird. But oh, how I loved my Becky. I knew I would have gone through any kind of pain to have my baby.

Nov. 8, 1970, a few hours before my 26th birthday and almost three months before our eighth wedding anniversary. Nearly eight years we had waited, being told we would never have a child, and now I was holding a miracle from God.

They wouldn't let Becky stay with me. The nurses explained she had to return to the nursery. I couldn't wait for feeding time, or when Jerry would come to see us. He brought flowers, candy, and cards for me and toy rattles for Becky.

Our home had always been filled with other people's children but now we were a family of our own _ four people bound in love. Jerry and I and our two children, Jeremy and Becky.

We gave Becky the nursery which had been decorated in pink and frills many years before. Jeremy moved to the guest bedroom which we decorated in blue for our little boy.

Caring for Becky was not quite the same as it had been for Jeremy. He was the perfect child, easily broken of bad habits, sleeping through the night, and never spitting up his milk. But Becky was the opposite, getting us up every 15 minutes during the night and spitting up half of her bottle. How many hundred times did I crawl under the bed for her pacifier? But how I loved both of them!

Jeremy and Becky both liked to be outdoors, to play with Mimi and the other poodles, Elle Mae, the German Shepherd, and Finky, our goat. But Jerry and I both felt we needed more room for the children.

I told him about a farm in Mayville my family visited when I was a small child. The 80-mile trip to my parents' friends seemed like it would never end but what fun we had when we arrived. I would roll up the legs of my overalls, and with my pigtails bouncing, I would race the other kids to run barefoot through fresh cow manure. I know it sounds disgusting but it was so much fun then.

46

I remembered helping gather eggs _ I looked for the tiny pullet ones that looked like bird eggs _ to go with the bacon frying on the wood stove. It smelled so good _ the memories were some of the best of my childhood.

Jerry and I talked about how great it would be to have a place like that for our children to grow up rather than be crowded in the subdivision even though we loved our neighbors dearly.

Then, Jerry walked in one day and announced we were moving to the country. He had worked out a deal with Al to help us with a down payment on a mini-farm in Howell, Michigan _ dairy farm country about 50 miles outside Detroit. It would also mean longer drives for Jerry to get to work but it would mean more freedom for our family.

"I'm tired of being cramped on a 60 by 120-foot lot. It's time to move from the city _ we're going to the country," Jerry said. He told me he had found three acres in Howell with an old rambling farmhouse.

"There's lots of fresh air, plenty of room for the children to play, plenty of room for our family to grow. There will be more to life there than seeing which neighbor I can beat in getting the grass cut each week or worrying about our children running out in the street."

Off to the country we went in 1971, a family of four.

"Are you crazy, woman?"

A year later, we were living on a little Old McDonald farm 50 miles from Detroit. We had a menagerie of animals that made our home seem more like Noah's Ark _ a goat, a lamb, chickens, ducks, a horse and a cow. The farmhouse was large and almost every weekend it was filled by visitors from the city. The "city children" loved hay rides, helping feed the animals, and milking the cows.

But something was missing from our lives. Even with two children of our own and all the visitors coming and going, that big farm seemed to have an empty space.

Jerry and I discussed at length becoming foster parents. We wanted to help other children who did not have families.

Based on our previous experiences in trying to adopt, I had not expected any cooperation when I called Catholic Social Services. But I discovered the Howell area was handled by the Lansing office rather than Detroit which had rejected us in the early days of our marriage. I found a friend in Barbara McKnight, the social worker, and she said they had two orphan Indian girls they could place with us immediately.

Rochelle, 13, and Luella, 11, came to live with us in the summer of 1972. Their Sioux Indian names had been Pearl Necklace and Renee Necklace respectively, and they were from the Rose Bud Tribe in South Dakota. Rochelle wore her waist length black hair loose while Luella often braided hers. About a year earlier, they had been adopted following the death of their parents _ their mother was killed in a traffic accident and their father died a short time later from high blood pressure _ but the adoption wasn't working out. We were asked to serve as a foster family for the girls until the problems could be resolved.

With each other, the girls were loving, always giggling and whispering. However, with others they only spoke when spoken to and then gave only yes and no answers. The girls also responded differently to Jeremy and Becky. Luella loved to play with the smaller ones and would rock Becky for hours. Rochelle, on the other hand, was friendly but spent very little time with Jeremy and Becky, preferring to ride the horses and be outdoors.

The girls tried to avoid household chores but I was convinced this would change in time. Perhaps their quietness and unusual behavior had something to do with their Indian background. It was for certain Jerry and I knew next to nothing about their native heritage. We decided to simply adjust to their needs.

About three months later, we learned that efforts to salvage the girls' adoptive home had failed. "Would we keep Rochelle and Luella permanently?" Barbara McKnight asked one day.

Of course we would. We were now a family of six.

"Jerry, we have a problem. Now Becky has older sisters but Jeremy doesn't have a brother."

I sometimes wonder if Jerry's heart for children is larger than mine. Without a moment's hesitation, he agreed we should adopt a brother for Jeremy.

A brother for Jeremy. After all these years, the words jump at me like a highway billboard. We never once questioned the road we were traveling down. Never once thought about the direction our lives were taking. Locating a brother for Jeremy just seemed the rational thing to do.

The next day I called Barbara McKnight and explained our desire. Two days later she called back. They had a 7-year-old brother for Jeremy. Wonderful! But there were some strings attached _ three of them as a matter of fact. Jeff had an older brother and two sisters _ John, Laurie and Renee.

Jerry's heart was big, but was it this large? How could I tell him I wanted this family of four. I decided on the direct approach.

Just like I had met Jerry in the driveway years earlier to tell him that I was going to have a baby, I decided to meet him in the drive when he arrived from work.

"Honey, you won't believe this. It's perfect. They have a brother for Jeremy. Seven years old. Isn't that great?" I asked with a mischievous grin across my face. "And the best part is, Jeff has an older brother and two sisters. What do you think?"

"Four? Are you crazy, woman?"

A family of 10

"Sandy, we can't handle what we've got."

Jerry was stunned. Yes, he wanted a brother for Jeremy but the size of this family was getting out of control. It had been more than six years before we had adopted Jeremy, and nearly eight before Becky was born. Two years later we added two Indian girls and now, I was asking to add four more.

But I was one step ahead of Jerry.

"Barbara is going to send out pictures of the children. Then we can see what they're like. Of course, she'll send us background details about the children too."

"Honey, have you lost your mind?"

A couple days later when the photographs arrived, Jerry started melting. The children were so cute, their hungry eyes, searching for someone to love them.

Jeff was the youngest at almost 7. Then there was John at 8, Laurie, 10, and Renee at 12. Their mother had died of leukemia in 1968 and the father was unable to care for them. He had finally relented to allow the children to be adopted, except for Alex, his oldest.

The clincher came when the social worker told Jerry they had been unable to find a family who would adopt all four children. The children would have to be separated.

"No way," Jerry said. "You don't separate children like that. We'll take all four ."

It was the spring of 1973. We were suddenly a family of 10.

"No, I don't want to go!" Renee screamed, kicking Jerry as he struggled to pull her hands from the towel rack. The other three had gone to the car without a fight but Renee, frightened and angry, had taken refuge in her aunt's bathroom.

"Renee, they have ponies and horses and cows on their farm," the social worker said, trying to coax her out of the bathroom.

"I hate horses," Renee fired back.

Jerry and Renee had clashed at first sight. Finally, he pulled her kicking and screaming from the house. I still have a vivid image of Jerry dressed in jeans, boots and a red and black plaid flannel shirt striding across the yard with Renee tucked under his arm like a sack of flour.

This was horrible. The other three children were seated in the back of the car sobbing. The poor things were frightened to death.

Despite our two visits before taking the children to live with us, there did not appear to have been any preparation for the move. They had been living with an aunt and her husband on a military base but he was being transferred and they were unable to keep the children. John had asked Jerry on one of the initial visits if he were Paul Bunyan. In their eyes, he was the largest man they had ever seen.

"Renee, no one is going to hurt you. Quit kicking!" Jerry yelled. He finally flopped her down in the back seat of the car and when she tried to jump out, he pushed her head back down so she wouldn't be hurt by the closing door.

Anyone who may have driven by the scene would have thought we were kidnapping the children. It took awhile for them to settle down once we arrived home but the protest had quieted considerably when it came time for dinner and they eventually fell exhausted into their beds, their anger spent for the time being.

This day _ March 3, 1973 _ was a nightmare. The size of our family had grown so fast. Maybe I had pushed too hard.

The confrontation continued for awhile, Renee protesting that she didn't want to be called Tucker at school. The four additions thought it was cool to be in a family with two Indian girls and two small children but they wanted to keep their own identity.

Jeremy and Becky were so small they couldn't understand all the excitement and just took up with the new children, wanting to play. They had a way of melting the hearts of the older ones when they reached their little arms to be held and rocked.

Jerry and I knew it would take time to convince our new children of our love. At first they tended to shrug off our affection. They argued that whatever they needed, they could obtain from each other. They were a family _ and they didn't need Jerry and I, they said. In time, though, the children gradually learned we cared for them. And they began to accept our love. Slowly, we became a family.

"Did you girls take a bath?"

"No, and we're not going to," Laurie fired back at me.

53

"Oh, yes you are. Either you take a bath on your own or I'm going to give you one."

"You wouldn't dare!" Laurie said. Luella smiled, enjoying the stand-off but a little unsure if her new sister was right.

I proceeded to march the girls to the bathroom and started the water.

"Undress and get in the tub."

"No way!" Laurie said, crossing her arms defiantly.

"Then I'll do it for you," as I reached to help them with their clothes. Suddenly embarrassed, they began to undress and finally got in the tub. I proceeded to scrub each one down and wash their hair.

Laurie fought like a wildcat, screaming and splashing. Before I was done, the whole floor was standing in water and running out into the hallway. But that was the last time I had to bathe them. Suddenly they knew how to do it on their own.

Renee was the leader of the four.

"I didn't have to come with you all. But I promised my Mom I wouldn't allow the family to be split up," Renee said.

But she took the role of being mother a little too far. For example, she would tell the others they could have hot chocolate only if she allowed it. I had to step in and let them know I was the one who determined what they ate and when.

Laurie had a hot temper _ one of the things we had to break her of was trying to kick down the doors when one of the other children tried to keep her out of a room. But Laurie had a heart of gold when it came to the animals. She had a deep love for them and often volunteered for the chores like feeding the animals.

Rochelle loved horses too, always wanting to ride. But for the most part, she and Luella stayed to themselves.

From time to time, one of their favorite lines would be

fired at us _ "You don't know what we've been through." But I refused to pamper them because they had led a hard life.

It was obvious the children did not understand responsibilities. We gave them chores to teach them _ No beds made. No television. No feeding of the animals. No dessert.

The four children one day confronted Jerry.

"You don't love us as much as you do the other children," Renee said.

"That's right," Jerry said. Renee jumped back, obviously not expecting that answer.

"Well, you can't expect us to love you as much as the others _ it's something that grows with time," Jerry said, reaching out stroking Renee's hair. At the same time, he pulled Jeff up to him. Then he added the clincher.

"You don't love us as much as you love your grandmother."

They all hung their heads and agreed. "We just don't want to do chores. We don't like making beds. Or doing the dishes."

But we remained firm with our discipline. And we gave them lots of hugs, reassuring them we did love them. And indeed, the love grew.

One day, Renee, who only two months earlier had been threatening to run away from home, was helping me with the dishes. She gave me a quick hug, said "I love you" and ran out of the kitchen.

And Laurie wrote us a poem.

"To Mom and Dad:

"How I Feel _

"I feel the warmth of two people caring for me.

"They taught me what was wrong and right.

"They opened up my heart and made me feel free.

"They opened up my eyes to a world that was bright.

"I Feel Great."
Laurie.
It had been a real boot camp for us.

Our large family started attracting attention and in May of 1973, the *Detroit Free Press* ran a news article on our "kid farm" complete with pictures of the children feeding the animals and doing other chores.

Neighbors and their children from our previous subdivision home in Livonia were frequent visitors. This was a help for the newly adopted children to see other children interacting with each other and the love that we had for them, too.

My sister Debbie and her husband, Jerry's brother Michael, liked the country so much they decided to buy a home nearby.

Debbie and I started a group in the Howell area called "For Love of Children." Our purpose was for adoptive parents to support each other and promote adopting older children who had been rejected by others. Debbie and Michael had two children, Mickey and Heidi.

In addition to all those activities and helping run the farm, I took on odd jobs like teaching ceramics in our basement to financially support our children. Another odd job I undertook with Debbie was to conduct a dog census for the county.

We would walk door to door asking how many dogs they had. The county was checking for registrations and occasionally we would find a dog kennel. We received 50 cents a dog and when we ran upon a kennel, we would become excited _ it might mean as much as $5 for each of us.

As we did our survey, I noticed I frequently was having to stop and use the bathroom at service stations. I began to worry and decided to check with a doctor.

Again, I met Jerry in the driveway.

"Guess what?"

"Oh no, what this time?" he asked with a grin on his face.

"It's happened again!"

We were about to become a family of 11.

With another baby on the way, Jerry began earnestly seeking a new home with more acreage. Since the Howell area was dairy farm country, land was priced too high for our income.

Jerry decided to travel north to look for land. We took the two Indian girls with us, to give them a little more needed attention _ our daily efforts had been primarily focused on resolving the problems with the four newcomers.

We ended up as far north as possible in Bemidji, Minn., the hometown of Paul Bunyan and at the headwaters of the Mississippi River. It was said this area received more snow than any other place in the country. I shivered, not as much from the cold temperatures, but the thought of my family being snowed in for an entire winter.

The two girls didn't offer an opinion on the 100-acre tract we found. They remained their quiet selves as we placed a $500 deposit on the property. Although nothing was said, I noticed how they liked the wilderness while running and picking choke cherries.

We returned home to place our mini-farm in Howell up for sale. Jerry wanted to be moved by the time our new baby arrived.

Another miracle baby

"Let me see the baby!"

The children's excited chattering reminded me of a flock of geese. Jerry and I beamed with pride as Jessica was handed around the room to allow each of the eight children to hold their new baby sister. They were making over her like a new puppy. Her arrival Feb. 9, 1974 brought a ray of sunshine into a bleak Michigan winter.

Just like Becky's delivery, Jessica's had been difficult, being born in a posterior position. When I went for a checkup a couple of weeks before my due date, the doctor discovered I was about 3 cm and decided to induce labor. He didn't want to chance missing a Valentine's Day party the next day.

After 24 hours of labor, I begged for them to do a C-section but instead I was given more Pitocin _ at dangerous levels I would later learn. My labor continued for a total of 42 hours _ I felt some justice for my pain since the doctor missed his party anyway.

Prior to my delivery, Jerry had gathered all the girls and explained to them the basic facts of life _ with red face, soft voice, and much stuttering _ and that someday they too, would become mothers. They were all excited about having a baby sister _ the fact they were all adopted except for Becky did not enter their minds.

Jessica's arrival broke down a lot of barriers between us and the latest adopted children. Suddenly they were no longer the new children on the block. They were family _ they had been there first and now there was a new baby to love.

"You now know how I felt when you came into the family," I explained. They had each adopted the baby into their hearts just as we had adopted each of them.

We were still living in Howell when Jessica arrived. To our surprise, our house failed to sell within the 90 days of our contract and we lost the $500 deposit in Minnesota. Despite a faltering economy, Jerry insisted on pursuing a new home with plenty of acreage.

Other than "Sesame Street" and "Mr. Rogers' Neighborhood," the only television programs Jerry allowed the children to watch were "The Waltons" and "Little House on the Prairie." We wanted our own Waltons' farm _ fields for the children to be able to run in, and trees _ lots of trees, a peaceful isolation.

Through the United Farm Agency, we contacted real estate brokers in Kentucky, Tennessee, and Virginia. John Tarter of Liberty in Casey County, Kentucky was the only one to respond. When we saw the price of wooded acreage from that area, we decided to pursue it.

My parents had eventually fallen in love with the

Howell countryside and moved to be near all the grandchildren, purchasing a house less than two miles from us.

My mother never took Jerry's plans of moving to a larger farm seriously, commenting "I told you so" when the deal fell through on the Minnesota land. As we began making other inquiries, I dreaded the prospect of telling her.

Another person who was taking Jerry seriously was Al. Jerry had worked his way back up to the top as Al's field manager, earning $500 a week plus expenses and he was provided with a new truck equipped with a telephone every year. Jerry supervised all the crews from trenching to pouring foundations and block work in the metropolitan Detroit area.

Al had lost Jerry once and he didn't want to risk it again. He offered Jerry $50,000 a year in salary, plus a new truck, and a percentage of the profits if he would stay. Jerry turned it down.

"I've had enough of the rat race. I've worked my way to the top twice and I'm still not happy, Al," Jerry said. "I want space for the children and to try my hand at farming."

When Al realized there was no changing Jerry's mind, he offered to buy a farm in Kentucky, build us a house, provide the best equipment and a new truck and a share of the profits.

On Memorial Day 1974, Jerry and Al flew down to Kentucky in Al's airplane to check out a 600-acre farm near Hustonville in Casey County. They flew back with Jerry announcing we were moving to Kentucky as soon as our house sold.

"Jesus loves me"

"Mommy, I want to sing my new song for you. May I?"

My three-year-old Becky and the other children had just come home from Sunday School at Oak Grove Methodist Church. Earlier in the week, a man had stopped in a big yellow church bus to ask if the children could come to Sunday School. Being Catholic, I wasn't familiar with what was meant by Sunday School but we thought it would be good for the children since we weren't going to church at the time. Also, it would give us a break on Sunday mornings _ with nine children in the home, a couple of hours for Jerry and I to have some quiet time would be a welcome relief.

As I looked down at my daughter with her blonde hair and shining blue eyes, Becky didn't look like she was big enough to be singing. But just like any other mother, I put down my dishtowel and sat down at the kitchen table to hear her song.

"Go ahead, Honey, sing."

"Jesus loves me. This I know for the Bible tells me so ..."

The words rang in my ears. I had never heard such a beautiful little tune. The songs from the Catholic choir of my youth had not haunted me like this. "Jesus Loves Me _" the songs of my youth had been mostly in Latin. "Jesus loves me, this I know _" Did I know it? I wasn't sure but my Becky's voice was as sweet as an angel's. Tears welled in my eyes.

"What's the name of that song, Becky?"

"Jesus Loves Me."

"Mommy, let me recite my Bible verse for you," Laurie said, tugging at my arm.

"Okay," my thoughts were far away. "Jesus Loves Me."

"John 3:16 _ For God so loved the world that he gave his only begotten Son, that whosoever believeth in him should not perish but have everlasting life."

My attention snapped back to Laurie. "Where did that come from?"

"It's from the New Testament. Let me show you which book." New Testament. Book. What was this child talking about?

Laurie picked up the big white Holy Bible I had on the coffee table. All the kids joined around while Laurie looked for the verse.

"Laurie, that's not the New Testament. That's the Bible." I had bought one for my coffee table, just like the one I remembered in my mother's living room as a child. But Mom's had only been for decoration. We never read the Bible _ as children we weren't even allowed to touch it.

"Don't be crazy, Mom. The Bible has an Old Testa-

ment and a New Testament," Laurie said.

One of the children piped up, "John 3:16 is in the New Testament." Laurie found it and handed the Bible to me.

Reading it slowly, I said, "That's nice, Laurie." My thoughts were a whirlwind of contradictions. Something completely new was happening. The bud of a new flower was beginning to form.

I started scanning the Bible while the children were gone to school and the younger ones were napping. When the children announced the church was presenting a special program where they sang and recited the Bible verses they had learned, we decided to go _ even my mother.

She was going to hear her Becky sing that song "Jesus Loves Me." I had her singing to everyone who stopped by the house. My father, a staunch Catholic, said there wasn't any way he would be caught dead in a Protestant church even if his granddaughter were singing.

I had never been in such a service. The children were singing their little songs and reciting their verses. There were no priests chanting in Latin to a congregation who didn't understand. There were no altar boys solemn in little white robes. Instead, a preacher offered a testimony on the rewards and pleasures of living a Christian life. I went home that evening humming the tune to "Amazing Grace."

In late July, we finally found a buyer for our little farm and began the monstrous job of packing. We only had 30 days. Since we had not located property in Kentucky to buy, John Tarter arranged for us to rent a farmhouse until we could find what we wanted.

"Sandy, you can't move away. We just moved up here a few weeks ago to be near you and the children. You can't do this to me," my mother shouted, her anger rising by the moment. But I assured her I would follow my husband to Kentucky.

Once again my mother was furious. She considered it a slap in the face that we were leaving after they had followed us to Howell from the big city. My father told her to leave me alone, that I had made up my mind and would never change it even though he thought I was acting on impulse. As for me, I couldn't understand why she was upset _ after all, my sister Debbie would be nearby and my two brothers, Pat and Perry, were still at home. I could remember when she had told me to stay out of her business when I was a teen-ager and had offered her advice. I now felt the same way _ she should stay out of my marriage.

But I remained upset. She refused to see me or talk to me on the telephone. I tried to get my mind off the confrontations with my mother by taking the children out one evening. As we were pulling back into the driveway, I saw Jerry coming towards me. What was he up to? I was usually the one who met him in the driveway. Was he reversing the trend? Was he going to tell me this time we were going to adopt more children?

But when Jerry reached the car door, I could see by his face this was not going to be news to rejoice about.

"Sandy, your mother has drowned."

Before I could make amends with my mother, she died in her bathtub.

Earlier in the evening, my mother had baby-sat for Debbie's new baby, Joey. After Debbie and Michael picked him up, Mom went to take a bath. Due to back problems, she was bathing on her knees in the tub. Apparently she had a coughing spell from her emphysema due to heavy smoking, went into shock, and collapsed face down in four inches of water.

Her death was traumatic for Debbie and me. As Polish Catholics we had been accustomed to going to funeral homes ever since childhood. My mother was a firm believer in grieving when a loved one, a friend or even a distant relative died, even if she didn't like them.

Mother had always wanted to be buried at the parish where she made her first communion. When Jerry and I went to arrange the funeral, we found the priest in his office, feet propped up on the desk and smoking a cigarette. Without moving an inch or putting down his cigarette, he said he could not allow her to be buried there. She had to be buried at the church in the parish near Howell where she had moved. My mother was lying in the funeral home and here was this man who called himself a man of God showing no compassion or understanding. His parting comment was that he was leaving on vacation and didn't have the time to work out anything.

We turned to our grandparents who had come to America from Poland as teen-agers to work in the factories. Grandma Mary, being from my mother's side, visited her priest to try to persuade him to grant my mother's wish. He still refused. I went to Grandma Burda on my father's side to see if she could arrange for my mother to be buried at her parish which was closer to my mother's former parish. At first, the priest said no, but after Grandma Burda slipped him a $100 bill saying it was a donation to the church, permission for burial was granted.

I left with a very bad taste _ I could not understand why my mother's wish could not be honored. Above all, I couldn't understand why or how money seemed to come into the picture when someone dies. It just didn't make sense!

The funeral was very hard on me. I couldn't imagine my children not having a grandmother, and above all, I couldn't conceive not having a mother. She was only 49 years old _ you just don't think of young people dying.

I fought with the decision to have an open coffin but Grandma Burda prevailed. I did not want to accept reality. I pictured my mother all swollen and black like drowning victims are. But when I saw her lying there, she was beautiful and peaceful looking. I cried in shame that we had parted with hard feelings. Then I wondered if she were in purgatory screaming with torment, waiting for her punishment to be fulfilled. We received several cards from friends who sent money to Catholic monasteries to pray her out of purgatory. I thought the rich could immediately pay their loved ones out of purgatory or hell _ was it fair?

After mother's funeral, plans for our moving speeded up.

Laurie was the most ecstatic about the move to Kentucky. She loved animals even more than Jeff and John _ the move south meant more room to play and more animals. Lu and Rochelle really didn't express any concern about the move but Renee fought it every step of the way. Her grandparents had been coming out to visit once a month and this would separate her from them.

But the children's father asked that we become guardian to their older brother Alex and take him to Kentucky with us. At 14, Alex had reached a point where his father could no longer control him and had ended up in a juvenile detention center.

When we agreed to take Alex, Renee had a change of heart about the move _ this meant the five would be together again.

Off to Kentucky we went. Me driving the van with all the children. Jerry with a U-Haul truck with all our belongings. Our animals came later on a truck _ the horses, the cow, chickens, two goats, the pony, and a lamb.

The children were excited as they saw the countryside, rolling pastureland and forests. We stopped overnight in Ohio to rest and plug in our freezer which was on the back of the truck with all our meat and frozen vegetables.

The farther south we went, along the road, I kept noticing unusual road signs.

"Jesus Saves."

"R-U-Born Again?"

"R-U-Saved?"

"R-U-Ready?" I wondered, ready for what?

The signs were tacked to fence posts and tree trunks, spray painted on bridges, even rock walls along the highways. I figured they were some sort of southern graffiti. By no means did I grasp their meaning.

"PAR-ER IN THE BLOOD"

"Mommy, someone is coming down the lane," I heard one of the girls yell, the screen door slamming behind her.

Company so soon? I was still trying to find some of my cooking pots from among the unpacked boxes. The house on Reedy Lane was not large enough to handle 10 children and all of our possessions from Howell. I had expected a bigger house _ two of the girls were having to sleep in the hallway, but I was trying to be patient. Jerry was looking for work and trying to locate a farm with ample space for all.

The rental house John Tarter had found on short notice was off Highway 501 on Grove Ridge, at the end of a lane named after the Reedys, an elderly couple who lived about a stone's throw away from our house. Company was unexpected.

"I bet it's a preacher, Mommy," one of the girls said, peeking from behind the curtains I had hung earlier in the morning in the small living room. "He's got a tie on."

"You guys behave now," I said, going to the door in response to the knock.

"Hi, my name is Terry Music. I'm the pastor up here at the little church on Grove Ridge, the Cornith Church of God," the preacher said. "I wanted to come by and introduce myself and invite you all to church."

I invited the preacher in. He appeared to be friendly and it gave me a break from unpacking. As he chatted, I thought of the little Oak Grove Methodist Church the children had attended before my mother's death.

"Do we have to wear dresses?" I asked.

"The women in our church wear dresses to the services and you all might be more comfortable if you did, but I want you to know you're welcome to come as you are," Bro. Music said.

Church. Yes, I said, we would send the children. I knew Jerry would agree. Since we were starting a new life, it would be good for the children to attend church.

"We don't want you to send your children, Mrs. Tucker. We want you and your husband to bring them," Bro. Music said. I promised him the children would be there.

The children couldn't get over the Kentucky hills _ our small farm in Howell had been flat land, and the children loved playing in the woods.

When we first arrived in Liberty, they were observing an annual town celebration, now known as the Casey Apple Festival. Renee panicked when she saw several women in long dresses like the characters from "Little House on the Prairie." Talk about going back into the country! We wanted a house like those on TV but this wasn't what Renee had in mind.

We settled the children down, explaining it was only

69

a special event. And even though the two Indian girls attracted a lot of stares, we had not had any bad reaction from the local residents. Jerry had cautioned the children _ he did not know what to expect in response to the girls' dark skin.

When Jerry returned from job hunting, he gave his blessing for the family to attend church. He took the girls and me to town where we found a second-hand store to buy blouses and skirts and dresses. Jerry insisted we respect the ways of the local folks since we were now a part of them _ even though it had been common to wear slacks or jeans to church in Michigan, we would not do it here.

Every dress and skirt had to be hemmed or altered. We went from tiny Renee just above 4 feet to Rochelle's 5-9 frame.

Sunday morning came and off to church we went _ all the girls in their best and only dresses, and the boys in their nicest jeans. The little church was only a mile away.

We took up the second and third rows on the right side with Jerry and I each taking the end of a row to help control the children. Our family of 12 appeared to equal about a fourth of the congregation. They opened their hearts and made us welcome, from Bro. and Sister Music to Lewis and Jewell Sims who lived across the road from the church to the "Porch Brothers" _ Albert and Carl Frederick, two elderly bachelors who lived on the main road at the end of the lane. Jerry had tagged the nickname on the two brothers because they were always on their porch waving to passing motorists.

Four small children _ close to Jeremy and Becky's age _ went to the front of the church and sang. Their singing touched my heart and I started crying, thinking back to little Becky singing "Jesus Loves Me." I had never seen anything like this in the Catholic Church. After Bro. Music preached awhile, he had an altar call for those who wanted to be saved.

70

I didn't understand what "saved" meant or what an altar call was but I sensed enough that I wanted to return. And we did. Sunday after Sunday.

It opened doors for us, ways for us to meet other people _ the family with all the adopted children. I guess we were a curiosity in the small community. Neighbors brought food and introduced themselves. Jerry started picking up odd jobs laying concrete block here and there while he continued to draw unemployment.

Then came the revival. What a revival was, I didn't know.

I was told it was like church for several straight nights in a row with an evangelist telling people how to be saved. That sounded interesting, but church every night! And what was saved? An image of the signs we had seen along the roads came to mind.

Jerry and I skipped the first night and let the children attend but when they came home all excited, we couldn't ignore their pleas to go the following night. When we arrived, the church was packed. Neighbors and people from other churches were there from miles around.

Alex and Rochelle had been promised they could go to a ball game at Casey County High School after the service. Renee couldn't _ she was being punished for smarting off.

"PAR-ER - there's PAR-ER in the BLOOD," shouted Bro. Charles Jones, the young evangelist from Anderson, Ind. His southern accent and his emotional "Power in the Blood" charges had me riveted to my seat.

"The blood of Jesus can cleanse you of your sins," the evangelist emphasized. "Belonging to the church ain't going to save you. It takes the Power in the blood."

What did he mean? I was a Catholic and I was going to Heaven. Sure, I had to spend time in purgatory to pay for my sins. What did he mean about being saved? And what's this "power in the blood?"

"Only the blood of Jesus, accepting the blood of Jesus to cleanse your soul of your sins and accepting Him in your heart as your personal savior is going to save you," he said. "You have to make a commitment and once you've made that commitment to serve Him as your master, you will be saved from the depths of hell."

He repeated "PAR-ER in the BLOOD" what seemed like a hundred times.

Over and over this man with the funny accent kept saying it took the "PAR-ER in the BLOOD" to save.

The rituals, the formality, the communion, the catechism classes, the priest who rejected my mother's burial request _ they all flashed through my mind. Wouldn't the priest be shocked if he could hear this young man talking about Jesus this way? Bro. Jones hadn't said anything about Jesus' mother Mary. He just kept talking about the power in the blood of Jesus.

It didn't make sense. If Jesus is love, and if it takes the blood of Jesus shed on the cross to cover our sins, and we don't accept that, we're not going to Heaven after all.

"I've been deceived all these years." I found myself thinking. "I'm going to hell if I don't give my heart and life to Jesus."

I saw people going to the altar, saying they wanted to accept Christ. How brave to take a stand like that, I thought. I started to squirm in my seat. I wondered if Jerry was feeling the same conviction.

Bro. Jones said if you wanted to be saved from eternal hell, "come down to this altar and accept Jesus into your heart and lives." The way he was talking, there was no amount of money or prayers that could get you out of hell. But pride kept me glued to my seat. Then the evangelist said, "If you are ashamed of Him, then He will be ashamed of you."

I saw my children, one by one, stepping out from behind their pews to go to the altar. My children, on their knees, saying they wanted to trust Jesus! It was like a magnet. I was drawn to the altar where my children were.

I had no control. The altar was full of people weeping, crying out for forgiveness of their sins. Through my tears, I saw Jerry had also come to the altar. We followed behind our children like sheep following the Shepherd.

Yes, there was POWER IN THE BLOOD and I had found it.

The Tucker Family, Christmas, 1974: Front row, from left, John, Jeremy, Becky, Jeff, and Laurie. Back, Renee, Alex, Jerry, Sandy with Jessica, Rochelle, and Luella.

The Galilean Home Family, Summer, 1989

BOOK TWO

Faith, Hope, and Room for one more
1974-1989

Noah's Ark _ Fall 1989

"Mom, help!"

I heard Oscar's plea as I walked through the babies' room but couldn't see our tiny four-year-old Guatemalan boy anywhere. Oscar is a doll whose smile creates dimples in his face deep enough you can bury your thumbs in, then watch his baby teeth flash brighter against his dark-complexioned skin and hear him giggle, "Don't do that."

Born with "frog legs," Oscar is recuperating from corrective surgery that will, in time, enable him to walk. His legs have been turned around and straightened _ it just appears he doesn't have kneecaps. He moves around clinging to an infant walker with wheels, or if he tires of that, he reverts to running on all fours like a miniature donkey.

"Mom, help!"

Oscar loves to play pranks. He is so small that he can hide in the most unusual places like the kitchen cabinets, but this plea sounds like a call for help rather than a game of hide and seek. The babies' room is for our bedfast children _ Oscar shouldn't even be in here.

I quickly scanned the room, trying to spot Oscar in one of the obvious places _ behind the wheel chairs or the rocking chairs for the babies. All 10 bedfast children are present _ from the blind sibling group of three to the two mentally retarded brothers from New York who must be harnessed in bed for their protection. The boys do not appear to have any sense of danger or express pain when they hurt.

Make that nine children. Christopher recently moved to Faith Mission Home in Virginia to receive specialized training for the educable mentally handicapped. When one of our children leaves, it still feels like they're here. Even Jeremy recently moving to Tennessee to work with a Mennonite builder or Becky leaving for Bible college.

"Where are you, Oscar?"

"Here, Mom."

I again heard Oscar's urgent plea, and this time, the sounds of the wheels of his walker on the vinyl floor. Turning, I realized the sounds were coming from the direction of the hospital beds where Baby Sandy and Ramsey are sleeping.

Baby Sandy came to us after she had been given up to die in Haiti, while Ramsey's mother was unable to handle his severe cerebral palsy. Both are confined to hospital beds which stand higher from the floor than the others. Today, the outside rail of each bed was extended within inches of the floor forming a "cage" underneath and between the two beds.

I bent down and looked underneath. Sure enough, there was Oscar pushing himself around, bumping his walker into the bedrails. His own private skating rink! The beds sit high enough off the floor that Oscar had strolled underneath while the bedrails were raised. Once they had been dropped, he had become trapped!

As I freed him from his "prison," Oscar lifted his little arms, flashed his famous smile, and said, "Mom, carry me." He has mastered English during the year he has been in our home. It will be heartrending to see him leave, just as it was for his Christian mother to let him come to America. My joy will be witnessing his mother rejoice when he arrives home, able to walk.

I lifted Oscar into my arms, chuckling at his predicament as I carried him into the family room where Elenue, our teen-ager from Haiti, was giving Sissy a sip of her juice. Sissy is the nickname Jerry has given to Baby Alicia, the spina bifida infant we had expected to arrive before our silver wedding anniversary more than a year and a half ago. Oscar spotted Sissy's juice and decided to get down to "share" it.

Thank You, Lord, for all these children from around the world. It has been like Noah's Ark around here during the last year and a half. The children keep arriving in twos and threes _ once we had seven to show up the same day! Back on our 25th wedding anniversary we had reached three dozen. By Mother's Day this year, that had grown to 63 in our home. Walking into the dining room that morning, I heard yells of "Surprise" and "Happy Mother's Day."

"Mom, You're The Best." Lord, that inscription on the balloon from Becky was so special. And so was Jessica's basket of carnations. She tore my heart out recently when she testified in chapel that she wanted to thank God she could share her mom and dad with all these other children.

Omar, our little Guatemalan boy with one leg shorter than the other, also brought me dandelions for Mother's Day. Candy, one of our little Mexican girls, gave me faded plastic flowers she "picked" at the cemetery up the lane from our home. Other gifts ranged from half-wilted flowers to green strawberries to cards drawn by the children at our Christian school. Berto, the boy we rescued from a children's prison in Haiti, presented me with a toothpick holder imprinted with a picture of Christ. Those special gifts only a child will bring _ gifts of love unspoiled by price tags and designer labels, gifts close to every mother's heart.

After oohing and aahing over each gift, wiping away tears, and sharing lots of hugs and kisses, it was time to help cook breakfast. I love cooking for my family _ I rarely have full kitchen control any more as the daily routine of running this growing home eats up my time. But on Mother's Day, a staff member had suffered a death in her family providing me with an opportunity to help prepare breakfast _ and lunch.

Meals are not an easy chore. For breakfast, we went through 15 dozen eggs, 200 large pancakes, and 10 pounds of bacon. Before the first bite was eaten, Jerry, as he has for years, read the children a Bible story, and prayed for daily guidance and thanksgiving.

At lunch, I led them in singing a song praising the Lord and as is our custom, one of the children led in prayer. Each day the children rotate saying grace at the noon meal.

It takes plenty of food for growing children plus our staff and visitors who eat with us. This meal included three 20-pound turkeys, five gallons of vegetables, 50 pounds of potatoes, a couple gallons of gravy, 20 pounds of dressing, and three gallons of banana pudding. Each day, we use six pounds of butter along with 20 to 25 loaves of freshly baked bread. And we go through 80 gallons of milk a week.

Cleanup is a whole different story. In almost all families, children are assigned dishwashing detail as part of their chores. But with 63 children, that's a lot of dishes and a lot of hands. In our home, chores are rotated weekly and posted on a list where it is most likely to be seen _on the

Oscar from Guatemala. (Photo by Jeremy Tucker)

refrigerator door!

Children from around the world keep coming _ two from war torn Afghanistan and seven from Guatemala just before Mother's Day. This summer Reinaldo from Brazil arrived. His life is in jeopardy as his curved spine presses against his lungs. More are on their way from Honduras, too.

We don't want to deceive anyone. Not every child in our home has become a success story but we continue to love and pray for them.

Luella, the youngest of the Indian girls we adopted so many years ago, called from a friend's home in South Dakota. She and her two boys, Joshua and Joseph, wanted to wish me a happy Mother's Day. Luella has straightened up her life and said Rochelle appeared to be off drugs too, and is getting her life in order.

John is nearing parole from a Montana prison. We're grateful to Lowell Bartels, whom we met at the national Caring Award presentation last year. He has been visiting John at Deerlodge Prison in Montana and in turn, John is starting to communicate with us again.

Renee has become a beautiful mother of two and Jeff is serving his country in the Army. Laurie, meanwhile, has broken contact with us but we have been told she loves her children dearly.

Nearly 15 years have lapsed since the night our children went to the altar in that small country church, the night Jerry and I trusted Jesus Christ as our personal Saviour. Lord, I didn't begin to understand what was happening to me that night but, oh, how I wanted to be forgiven of my sins, to know about the POWER IN THE BLOOD. I felt as though I shed enough tears to fill a river, Lord, and I was so full of joy, as if I were floating above the highest hill in Kentucky.

We've had our ups and downs, stumbled along the way, but You have always picked us up. Despite our trials and tribulations, life seems to grow sweeter each day.

Looking back, I realize those 10 children Jerry and I had when we came to Kentucky were to meet the selfish desires of our heart. After we accepted You into our hearts,

Lord, we discovered we wanted children to bring glory to You. We believe You called us to care for the least of these by taking in children others don't want or couldn't handle. Those who are handicapped mentally or physically, abused _ some abandoned by their parents. Others are here from Third World countries for medical treatment.

More than 150 have come our way during these last 15 years. With each child, we have tried to share the love of Jesus Christ.

We have seen our first child _ our adopted son Jeremy _ trust Christ as his personal Saviour. He jokes about being "the first and the worst," but his adoption paved the way for children who led us to You. Jeremy works in construction but talks of when he can become a missionary.

We shuffle to make room for more children. Even chubby Sissy who now fills that empty crib we had on our 25th wedding anniversary. Sissy's bed ended up in our room but Jerry doesn't mind. Each morning we awaken to her bright smile and the sound of her baby giggles.

Other beds have been moved into my former midwife clinic. The clinic is now located in the larger cabin attached to our house where our "adopted" Granny Elmer lived. She has moved to New York with her son who has retired.

This extra room for the clinic has been needed for a long time. Back at our anniversary, I had been involved in 115 deliveries of children, primarily in our neighboring communities, but that number is now nearing 200. And I feel like I'm a mother to them all.

Thank You, Lord. I confess I'm tired but I wouldn't exchange this peace and love in my heart for anything. What a trying, but exciting journey it has been since we came to know You!

Where love abounded

Pond Ridge.

It was known to our neighbors as the old Charlie Gorley place, but to me, it was the most beautiful 26 acres God ever created. From the rolling pastures to the two-story white frame home on a knoll overlooking a beautiful valley, to the two-tier waterfall on Mill Creek bordering the back of our farm.

Pond Ridge.

It was here we were baptized while friends and neighbors from the country church lined the holly covered banks of the creek; the waterfalls cascaded gently, splashing against the rocks and coming to rest where the country church pastor buried us in a watery grave to symbolize the death, burial and resurrection of our Lord and Saviour Jesus Christ. I can still feel the coolness of the water, the joy I sensed as my tears flowed, and the songs I heard as those lining the banks praised

God. They were singing what they called old-fashioned gospel hymns but it was new music to me and my soul.

Pond Ridge.

It was here Jerry tried to support our family, grubbing out a living and loving every minute of it despite the meager income he generated. The farms portrayed on television's "The Waltons" and "Little House on the Prairie" may have been larger, but this was our kingdom where the children could run and soak up the sunshine, where they could learn honest work and then taste the fruits of their labor.

Pond Ridge.

It was here that our home grew in Christian love, where love truly abounded in our hearts. I had a red heart painted in the eave of the house to symbolize the love. It was in this home we struggled in our growth in God, where we witnessed the birth of our first grandchild, and saw our family grow to 21 children.

Looking back, I can understand Jerry's excitement the day he burst into our rented home on Reedy Lane, announcing he had located a farm we could buy on land contract. When the children saw the property, they too fell in love with it. Especially the waterfalls on Mill Creek _ the name had come from a former flour milling operation. Many of the millstones still dotted the creek bank.

The children pitched in with the remodeling. Ripping old wallpaper from the walls. Scraping blistering paint. Repainting. Scrubbing. More scrubbing. And when the children were exhausted, they would race to the swimming hole at the bottom of the waterfalls for a quick dip.

It was home. Our home.

We moved during the spring of 1975. Alex, however, was no longer with us. He had returned to Michigan when we visited family at Christmas.

83

Alex had become a troublemaker at school, once pulling a knife on a teacher. Our relationship ended when he threatened me with a butcher knife.

Jerry had not yet arrived home from work when Alex came to me in one of his "Mother, I love you" moods. As I was preparing supper, he wrapped his arms around my waist and asked if he could go to town. When I told him he would have to wait and ask Jerry, he lost his temper. Alex picked up an eight-inch butcher knife from the counter and came at me.

I escaped out the front door by the grace of God. Alex did not follow; instead he ran out the back way and went to town. When confronted by Jerry later, Alex melted, swearing he didn't mean any harm. Alex had a loving side but after that incident, I couldn't trust him.

At Christmas, we returned Alex to his father but he apparently ran away later and ended up in trouble. Lord, we hear Alex was released from prison recently and is doing okay. And we understand his father has overcome his alcoholism and has been off the bottle for years. We praise You, Lord, for that!

After moving to Pond Ridge, Jerry applied for a loan to purchase 30 head of dairy cattle. We were turned down _ not because we asked for too much money but because we planned too small of an operation. If we had wanted into farming in a big way _ like a million dollars _ they would consider it. But 30 cows and nine children on 26 acres were all we needed _ that wasn't enough for the bankers, though. Since we couldn't afford the cows, we decided to raise pigs and grow peppers and pickles. Jerry picked up odd jobs around the county laying concrete block and driving our van to transport neighboring members of an old horse and buggy Mennonite order.

For the most part, the children loved the farming life,

Jeremy, Sandy, and Jerry in front of Pond Ridge home.

especially Laurie. She was the first one in the garden or to clean out the manure in the barn stalls. All this while her sister Renee was in the house painting her fingernails.

Renee's idea of being physical was doing cartwheels on the lawn or mowing the grass on Saturdays for the "Porch Brothers" to earn a little extra money to spend at Jack and Ethel Wright's Grocery. But get dirty? Never!

Wright's was the local general store _ just like on "The Waltons" on TV _ everything from food to work clothes, all crammed into a small concrete building. Shopping was a big treat for the children, especially for candy or ice cream. Ethel had Jack to place the nail box, filled with all sizes of nails for the customers, in front of the candy counter. This way, the smaller children could stand on the nail box and reach their favorite candy.

Jack had a pool hall next door to the grocery but Jerry didn't allow the children to even peek in the windows.

Tobacco became another taboo.

We only grew tobacco one year. Always unsure about the moral grounds of raising tobacco, we went ahead with it once since some members of the small country church were growing it. Laurie, who had picked up the nickname "Tank," would go to work in the tobacco patch wearing a T-shirt that said "Your smoking is hazardous to my health." If we weren't careful, this tomboy would have her bra hanging out of her jeans' pocket like a slingshot rather than wearing it.

Although intended as a work animal, Zebadiah, was the favorite family pet. This mule stood 17 hands high and would kneel and wait patiently while a half dozen children piled onto his back. When Jerry took the children for a hay ride, Zeb pulled a green wagon with red wheels. In the winter months, it was a huge sled loaded with laughing, squealing children.

Zeb was a very real part of our family and the children were grief stricken when he died with a tumor on his lungs. After the mule's death, we bought Mike and Nellie, two work horses which were taught voice commands to pull the wagon as we picked corn. Even though we bought a few cows along the way as our family grew, Josie who came with us from Howell, remained our favorite.

One winter when they were snowed in from school for five weeks, Jerry would place all the children on a sled and use the work horses to pull it down the hill by Grandpa and Granny Sims.

Mr. and Mrs. Thelmer Sims _ they were always Grandpa and Granny to us _ their house became a favorite visiting place for the children. Their house was just down the lane, in view of ours. If I couldn't find one of the children, I knew where to look first, particularly for the smaller ones who would sneak off to Granny's to see all her birds chirping in their cages. Granny always had peanut butter and honey sandwiches for the children. Jeremy had to be a little different _ he would go to Granny's and ask for an egg sandwich. Naturally, she would oblige.

Jeremy was Granny's favorite. He was at her house about every day "until he growed up," playing in the outbuildings where Grandpa stored his tools.

Granny also kept an eye out for any of the little ones who strayed off from our home. One day she found Jeff crying in her front yard. She couldn't get him to stop; he apparently had fallen in the gravel lane.

Finally she asked, "Jeff, are you a man or a mouse?"

"I'm a mouse and I want to go to the house," Jeff sobbed.

We laughed about the incident later when Granny told us. The Sims were so special to us _ one year at Christmas, I gave Grandpa a Bible. You would have thought I had given him a million dollars!

After Jerry removed our telephone, the Sims were our contact with the outside world. He had become frustrated with the teen-age girls fighting to use the phone. Jerry felt they should be outside enjoying the sunshine rather than wasting their time in meaningless chatter. The phone came out and the Sims allowed us to give out their number in case of emergencies.

Late one evening in the summer of 1975, Grandpa Sims knocked on our door. A state trooper stood quietly by him.

"Jerry, your brother has drowned."

Death of a loved one

Jerry told the children to turn down the television when he heard the knock. Company was a special treat and we all crowded around as he opened the door.

Hearing the tragic news, the children dropped to their knees in prayer and cried. Michael had drowned in a pond during a picnic outing celebrating his birthday.

Jerry borrowed money from Grandpa Sims for the trip to Michigan and we awoke the Wrights at the grocery store to gas up our van.

It had been a year of tragedy for my sister Debbie _ the sudden loss of our mother, a miscarriage, and now the death of her husband. She was left with three small children _ Mickey, Heidi, and Joey. No insurance and she hadn't worked in six years.

There was no one in Howell to turn to. Dad wasn't able to care for them. We insisted on "adopting" Debbie and her family, and she agreed. Over night our family grew by four.

Debbie found work as a waitress at the Somerset Holiday Inn before winter set in and later became food manager at the Danville Holiday Inn. Eventually Debbie bought a small brick home at Waynesburg not far from our farm at Pond Ridge. She and her children were constant visitors at our home. We continued to care for her children six days a week while she worked. They were around our home so much that Joey called Jerry "Daddy."

Jerry's biggest aggravation was all the teen-age boys who came up our driveway (we lived at the end of the lane) to see all the Tucker teen-age girls.

In a weak moment, we had allowed Rochelle, the oldest, to have a date. This became a sore spot with Renee who also felt she should be able to date even though she was much younger.

One day following one of our confrontations with them about boys, I noticed an article in The Lincoln County *Interior-Journal* newspaper. There was a picture of a young man named Mark (not his real name), an honor student at Lincoln County High School, who had been accepted as a Mormon missionary. The story said upon graduation, Mark would serve the church at his own expense for two years as a missionary.

I showed Jerry the picture of Mark in his white shirt and tie _ an All-American boy image. Jerry waved the newspaper in the girls' faces.

"Why can't you girls find a decent boy like this instead of the bums that try to come up this driveway?" Jerry asked.

Lord, the devil had sowed the seeds of deception.

The following day I called the Mormon church. We

wanted so desperately for our family to be happy, to be a true Christian family. The emphasis the Mormons placed on family togetherness seemed what we needed. But we failed to have on the full armor of God _ we didn't carefully search out the doctrine of the Mormon church.

After my call, two Mormon missionaries visited, and Mark from the newspaper clipping, was with them. Mark was an immediate hit with the children. They would help him in his greenhouse and he often stayed over at our farm.

Lord, when we were first saved, I would soak up Your Word like a sponge. The folks at the little country church couldn't seem to answer all the questions I had about the Bible, but the Mormons always had answers for whatever I fired at them. Of course, that was the wolf in sheep's clothing. They hooked us and then slowly pulled us into their boat.

I was always curious whether God replaced the apostles as they were killed off. My Sunday School teacher didn't have an answer for me. When I heard the Mormons had apostles in their faith, I considered this proof that they were of God.

We allowed the missionaries into our home to instruct us in how to live as Mormons. Monday nights we observed Family Home Evening, bringing all the children together and sharing as a family unit _ reading Bible verses, singing, and ending with one of the children praying. During these evenings, we also discussed any family problems.

Mormons encourage large families. We already had one but decided to become a foster home, to help even more children. With my sister's three children who moved in with us after their father's death, and the foster children, we grew to 21 at our little farm.

Taking in foster children was an act of love, but it brought trouble into our home. They were so precious, at times, Lord, but they came from varying backgrounds and had numerous problems, many of which we were not prepared to handle.

There were three redheaded brothers - Jimmy (who looked like Huckleberry Finn with a deep southern accent), Jeff (we called him Silas since we already had a Jeff), and Ricky, who had freckles.

And there was Nancy, who came from a rough moral background and was a couple of years older then Renee.

Another foster child was Steve, 12, who was always stealing anything he could get his hands on when your back was turned. Finally he left our home and was placed in a treatment center where he ran away, stole a delivery truck and went on a reckless driving spree before he was apprehended.

Carolyn, arrived at the age of 17 with her baby, Laura Mae, a year and a half old.

Cathy and Laura were two sisters who didn't know how to eat a meal or didn't want to take a bath. One day, the girls had come home and discovered their mother overdosed on drugs. They were with us a short time before moving to live with an aunt out of state.

Lee, who looked like the cartoon character "Mister Magoo," was a chubby two-year-old but still looked like a seven-month-old baby. He was nearly bald and cross-eyed and wore thick eyeglasses. "Cookie" was the only word he could say.

When the social worker brought Elizabeth, two, she handed her to Renee. The child was soaked with urine dripping into her shoes. I went to change her diaper and screamed thinking her intestines were falling out. It turned out the child had roundworm.

The child's mother had given her a pack of hot dogs to eat before walking out of her life. Apparently not used to running water, Elizabeth would become hysterical in the bathtub. She slept in a crib by Renee's bed and Renee would often wake to find Elizabeth banging her head against the wall.

In the months we had lived at Pond Ridge, we had become more than pig farmers. Jerry had Jacob Peachy, an Amish man in Pennsylvania, paint a sign for us that read "Tucker's Home for Children" and "Missionaries Welcome."

Jerry was always taking the Amish and Mennonite neighbors different places in our van and he picked up the sign on a trip north. Renee _ always primping over her hair and clothes _ went along on that trip, happy to get away, but fussing that the two crates of chickens they were delivering were messing up her clothes.

At times, we had up to eight missionaries staying at our home. Jerry added two bedrooms and a bath to our house to care for the additional children and visitors.

Once we had to repair a water line from our spring, and when Jerry replaced the sidewalk, he inscribed verses of Scripture. One was: "Except a man humble himself and become as a little child, he shall in no wise enter the Kingdom of God."

I gave up my coffee (caffeine wasn't allowed), no more chocolate and we gladly tithed as required by the Mormons. We started attending services at the Mormon church in nearby Danville. Jerry had started a beard before we became Mormons and some of the folks called him "Brother Brigham" after Brigham Young, a leader of the Mormon movement in America.

Jewell Sims _ she and her husband Lewis treated our family to dinner numerous times after church services at First Cornith _ was always teasing Jerry about his beard.

The girls, except for the older adopted ones, and I quit wearing pants before becoming Mormons. After seeing the other women at the church in their dresses, Jerry felt we should dress that way also _ not only on Sunday but every day of the week.

When we joined the Mormons, it was easy to adhere to their rules _ we didn't smoke or drink. Smoking had always been repulsive to me. My parents were such heavy smokers it always made me sick, especially at the dinner table.

Our television set _ I should say sets _ came out of the house before we joined the Mormons. With all of our children, it was difficult to get everyone into a single room. Jerry had removed a wall separating two rooms to make a large living room and placed the heating stove in the center. This blocked the view of some children watching television. The remedy was to get a second TV and place one at each end of the long room _ programmed to the same show.

However, one morning Debbie and I were watching a television program with a news feature on breast cancer. To our shock, they were showing a woman in a shower actually examining herself.

I turned down the sound of the TV, called Jerry into the house and asked him what he thought of the program. He had stopped in the doorway, resting his hands against each side of the door jam. His face colored with anger, his hands pushing against the door frame. As I heard the creaking of the door jam, I thought of the story of Samson and the temple pillars from the Old Testament.

Jerry unplugged both televisions, took them out and destroyed them before the children arrived home from school.

After becoming Mormons, Jerry was allowed to baptize our children at our waterfalls. Some of us had been baptized there earlier after we had been saved at the little country church. However, as Mormons, we were required to go through their baptism ritual.

Lord, remember that Christmas letter I wrote to our

friends in December of 1976? It reflected how seriously we were taking our Mormon faith.

Jerry had just been ordained a priest. Renee was taking a seminary class in the New Testament. John, at 12, was a church deacon, and Jeff, an honor student at 11, was talking of becoming a missionary. Three foster children were also involved: Jimmy, 14, was an ordained teacher, and Silas and Steve, both 12, were deacons. All of the boys were active in the Scouts which is encouraged by the Mormons to build character.

And we set aside food, water and grain. The Mormons believed they would have to go through the Great Tribulation _ these essentials would allow us to survive.

Life has to have its fun moments. Once when a young Mormon missionary was starting out, Jerry and another missionary we knew decided to "break in" the new fellow.

For many of the missionaries who stayed with us, our rugged country was a new experience. Our missionary friend told the young man he had heard Jerry was a "backwoods heathen" and he didn't know what to expect when they came to visit.

We let the children in on the gag. After the missionaries were in the house, Jerry stomped into the living room in his oldest overalls, his beard and hair messed up, and carrying a big whip. On cue, the children ran out of the room, screaming, "Don't whip me." As they peeked around the corner, they saw the new missionary dive out an open window in the living room and take off running for dear life.

The young man was so frightened he almost went back on his commitment to the mission field. I don't think we ever convinced him he had been set up for a practical joke.

All of our children were expected to pull their share of

the load when it came to chores, even the foster children. But some of them weren't used to work, especially as hard as we emphasized our work ethics.

I remember the summer we raised cucumbers and peppers _ five acres of them, getting a penny a pound for all our hard work! Of all the projects we tried to keep food on the table, I hated this one the most. Being reared a city girl, I wasn't used to this type of physical labor. The heat and bending almost did me in, not to mention the dirt and sweat bees that got under my clothes. But I had to set an example for the children _ I stayed in the field. From daylight to dark _ in the dust and the mud we worked _ going to bed each night bone tired and rising at daybreak to begin again.

And those foster children who believed it was their right not to work never ceased to complain. Eventually they conceived what they believed was a quick solution to their problem. One of them made a call to the state, claiming we were violating child labor laws, while the others backed that child up with stories of long hours in the fields. An investigation followed of allegations we believed had been made by an outsider. We were cleared, never knowing the truth until years later, when in a moment of reminiscing about her childhood, Renee confessed to being one of the leaders of the "Pepper Patch Revolt."

For some time it had been obvious to Jerry and I that Rochelle was troubled but there had not been any hint as to the problem. Finally one day she approached Jerry with a tearful confession.

"I'm going to have a baby."

Trouble in this world

Jerry and I suffered a private pain as only You know, Lord, as we struggled to help Rochelle _ hurting for her and with her. We had tried so desperately to raise our children to do Your will. How had this happened to a Christian family?

Rochelle's confession was shocking but not a complete surprise. She had earlier left home with a young man, telling Jerry they were going to marry. Weeks later, Rochelle returned after discovering he was already married.

Of course, Jerry and I forgave Rochelle and welcomed her home.

Rochelle stayed in school, completing her senior year. She was able to conceal her condition since she was tall and used to wearing baggy clothes.

Since we couldn't afford and didn't have insurance, Rochelle agreed for Betty Davis, a nurse, to serve as her midwife. Just before midnight on August 23, 1977, Rochelle gave birth to a baby girl.

That night, we rang a school bell to let Grandpa and Granny Sims know the baby had arrived. They dressed and came up the lane in the darkness of the night to see Your newest miracle, Sunshine. They held the newborn baby even before she had been dried off.

Rochelle, 19, was young, a child herself. Motherhood didn't impress her. Once the baby was born, Rochelle began staying out again, away from home for days. She treated Sunshine like a new puppy, and at best, a little sister.

We couldn't see raising Sunshine as our own and risk Rochelle moving away years down the road, taking Sunshine with her. We approached Rochelle about allowing us to adopt Sunshine. She agreed. Here I was, age 32, and a grandmother. We helped Rochelle buy her first car and after that, she pretty much lived her own life.

But our troubles with the older children were not over.

After moving to Pond Ridge, on the Lincoln-Casey County line, the children went to Lincoln County High and Waynesburg Elementary rather than Casey High and Middleburg.

Renee didn't do anything on a small scale. Everything was very dramatic and enlarged out of proportion. Her first day of high school was business as usual. Renee came down the stairs carrying a suitcase containing a couple sets of clothes.

I confronted her and she responded, "Well, you don't think I'm going to my first day of high school and wear the same outfit all day do you?" The suitcase went back to the bedroom and Renee went to school. To my embarrassment, I later discovered she talked other girls at school into exchanging clothes between classes.

When Renee was about 15, she ran away with a black boy who had a feather in his cap for every white girl he dated. When we found her, she had been missing three days.

By this time, we begun questioning public schools _ at 12, Jeff had told us about a girl in his class who was going to have a baby. We heard the public schools were handing out contraceptives, having sex education classes, and promoting abortion without the consent or knowledge of the parents.

We took Renee to a state social worker for counseling. She argued and yelled all the way. "I can't wait until I'm 18 and can do what I want to do."

We told the worker how Renee had been rebelling. We explained that we weren't concerned about the boy's color _ Jerry and I both had black friends in Michigan _ the fact was we didn't want our daughter running around with any boys especially with such a reputation as he had.

"Well, what's the matter? Are you prejudiced?" the worker asked as we sat in shocked dismay. "She's 15 years old. Don't you think she can make choices for herself?"

"What if something happens?" I said. "She's just a child."

His response: "That's what birth control is for."

That was the last time we went to him. He was not concerned about our values _ he was trying to destroy our family, not help us. Renee settled down somewhat but we had to keep a tight rein on her.

That summer we allowed Renee to visit her grand-mother. She told Michigan school officials she had been reared in an Amish family, lied about her age, and then took and passed a GED test.

Compounding our image of public schools was the language Jerry encountered while driving a school bus one term. He was shocked at the profanity he heard and became

98

concerned over the effect it was having on the little ones.

We began considering removing our children from public schools and building our own, like our Mennonite neighbors.

In the spring of 1978, we visited a Mormon temple in Washington, D.C. As You know, Lord, when we tackle something, we go full force. No holding back. No doing it halfway.

A visit to a Mormon temple requires a recommendation from a bishop or a regional stake president. We were considered to be living "righteous" enough to receive a "temple recommend" in a relatively short time, rather than the number of years it takes many Mormons.

We traveled to Washington where our marriage was "sealed for eternity." And we were "sealed for eternity" to our children. All of the ceremonies were very ritualistic, requiring us to wear "sacred garments" under our "sacred" white clothes.

Somehow, I didn't feel right even as we went through the rituals. Luella's family history was being questioned for some unknown reason. A message was sent to the Mormon prophet in Utah to talk to God and then have the prophet call back to the temple. I had not heard of such goings on before and I began to question this religion. Finally, the prophet called, saying God had okayed Luella's inclusion. How this transpired I didn't know but I knew you couldn't just call God on a telephone _ the whole matter upset me.

At the temple, we watched a film presentation on the history of the Mormon church. Adam was portrayed as God _ I could not picture God as ever having been with sin. There was also an explanation of the baptism of the dead where Mormons were to be baptized for their deceased relatives so they might be saved in the spiritual world. And then they were saying that after our deaths, in effect, Jerry would become a savior of some planet unknown to us at that time, and I would become one of his goddesses.

I could not believe what I was hearing! But I dismissed it as the devil confusing me rather than the Holy Spirit trying to warn us.

We returned from Washington disturbed by what had transpired. Our concern grew as the local Mormons questioned our decision to pull our children out of public school and start our own. Our children would only attend up to the eighth grade as our Mennonite neighbors did.

The Mormon philosophy was that you were to pursue education because it helped you to financially prosper. The emphasis on prosperity at any cost began to rub Jerry the wrong way and we began questioning if the Mormons were for real.

In the summer of 1978, we decided to pursue building our own school in the field behind our home. However, we encountered opposition which would not permit us to open. We didn't want to put our children through a legal battle when we could move away peacefully.

Jerry took Jeff and Jeremy with him to visit Ora Miller, an Amish man in Montana he had been corresponding with through the national Mennonite-Amish newspaper, *The Budget*. They returned _ the boys excited about their big adventure of seeing the West and Jerry announcing we were going to Montana.

An auction _ all of our possessions were at the mercy of the auctioneer's gavel. Jerry's power tools. My furniture. Even Josie, the family cow we had brought from Howell, Mich.

That fall day in 1978 we were saying good-bye to "the world." We were selling our material possessions and taking our children to Montana where they would be safe _ isolated from "the world." Maybe this way they wouldn't end up in trouble like Rochelle and Renee. Both of the girls were going back to Michigan, Rochelle to her former adoptive mother and Renee to her grandmother's.

No more would we hear children's laughter in this home where love had abounded. No more summer picnics or fried chicken dinners out on the front lawn. Nor would we see the orchard which Jerry had planted in the spring, bear fruit.

The auction lasted into the night as Berkley Sayers went full blast until everything was sold. His voice becoming raspy from exhaustion _ it was the largest auction he had ever had in Lincoln County.

Somewhat reluctantly, my sister Debbie agreed to relocate her family too. We had always been close and she didn't want to be left in Kentucky alone. We would be company for each other during the long days Jerry would be in the mountains building our log home.

We had been a fine Christian family until the children entered high school; after that Jerry had been unable to maintain the children's respect. We blamed the public school system for our losing control of our children.

In Montana, life would be on our terms and our family would grow strong in the peaceful mountain atmosphere. We planned to live simply _ no more conflicts.

Good-bye world

When a violent snowstorm forced us off the road for
the night as we moved to Montana, I should have known
"leaving the world" was not an escape to the Promised Land.
Our attempt to shield our family from worldly ways turned
into a year full of disappointment and heartache.

That year we left the Mormons, accepting the reality
of having been deceived. We encountered rejection by our
neighbors. And it was the year our adopted son John became
a lost sheep.

Sure, there are some good memories.

Watching John, Jeff, and Jeremy helping Jerry build
our log cabin. Becky, Jessica, and Sunshine constructing a
snowman and helping me bake homemade bread. Luella and
Laurie accepting responsibilities for babysitting Debbie's
children while she worked as a waitress.

To our surprise, the Amish who lived in the desolate

area refused to sell us property since we were Mormons. I guess they could not understand why anyone would intentionally want to live like a pioneer, to give up luxuries like electricity, telephones, and indoor plumbing to live as they did.

We finally located an English man who sold us his 100 acres of mountainous land which had formerly been a Christmas tree farm. It was located in northwest Montana in the Rexford area of the Kootenai National Forest. Only one tract of property separated us from the Canadian border.

Debbie found an apartment in Kallispell, about 120 miles from Rexford. We stayed with her while Jerry and the boys built our log cabin. They would return to the apartment each weekend.

Ora Miller and his older boys felt obligated to help us build our log cabin since he had encouraged us to move out there. It snowed every day and that log cabin on the mountain began to take shape while the curious Amish skeptically stood back in wonderment.

In northwest Montana, the wind rarely blows so the snow falls in big, fluffy flakes and piles high on every post, mailbox, even the clotheslines. The Ponderosa pine trees bend their limbs to the ground under the weight of the snow. The mountains and the valleys look like marshmallow frosting. I always looked forward to the menfolk coming back to Kallispell on the weekends. We were anxious to hear of the progress made on the cabin.

I roared with laughter when Jerry told me of Jeremy, then 9, having an accident due to a flu bug. He said he had to take his pants off and stand him outside and wash him with snow.

On Christmas Eve 1978, we moved into our new home. It was 20 degrees below zero, the wind howling through the cracks of the logs in our cabin. It was paradise to Jerry while the children and I nearly froze.

At the last moment, I asked Jerry if we could decorate a Christmas tree. He protested. We had become aware the Amish and Mennonites did not observe the traditional Christmas tree, feeling it was a sign of vanity. They defend their stand by the Scripture in Jeremiah 10 that refers to a tree decorated in silver and gold as being a vain, heathen practice.

Jerry was taking their interpretation seriously. He was even disturbed that our property had once been utilized as a Christmas tree farm. Reluctantly he cut off the tip of a standing tree, and nailed a board to the bottom of it for me. The children helped me decorate it with pieces of tin foil.

Knowing time and money would be in short supply after our move, I had done my Christmas shopping for the children before we left Kentucky and carefully hid the packages away.

On Christmas morning, after the children had opened their gifts, Jerry yanked the tree up in one hand and told me to "Kiss it good-bye." This was the last Christmas tree we have ever had in our home.

The Amish began to realize we were serious about our move to Montana. They began accepting us _ even allowing our children to attend their school.

My biggest adjustment was doing without necessities like a microwave oven, a freezer, and my vacuum cleaner. I had dreamed I would actually miss a vacuum cleaner. Our wood stove turned out to be too small to heat our cabin. A neighbor, Roman Schlabuch, and his son, Deon, discovered us one morning nearly frozen. He loaned us one of his larger wood stoves and helped Jerry place plywood over our plank floor. Cold air was pouring through the cracks in the floor making it almost impossible to retain any heat.

Jerry and the girls in front of the Kootenai General Store.

The Amish came to our rescue one Sunday when a forest fire broke out near our cabin. They had just dismissed church when the flames were spotted. Here they went in their black suits with stand-up collars and collarless shirts fighting the blaze with blankets or whatever could be found and digging firebreaks with shovels.

One of the strangest sites to get used to was all the mule deer that came near our cabin, apparently unafraid of the humans who had invaded their kingdom. A mule deer is a large, slow moving animal, about twice the size of a normal deer with floppy ears like a mule. One morning we awoke to find the enormous gentle face of a mule deer peering into our window. It turned out he was only one of a herd of about 50 in the clearing around our cabin.

During the winter, the boys cut ice out of the lake.

Horses and wagons hauled it up to the cabin where we stacked it between the pine trees and piled sawdust on top _ we had ice all summer, even during 110 degree days.

And the boys enjoyed catching brook trout by the dozens and camping for a weekend in the mountains, always keeping an eye open for bears. For them, it was one great adventure.

Our cabin finished, we built a store at the foot of the mountain for the Amish community. Seven Amish families invested $1,000 each to stock the Kootenai General Store since we didn't have the money. It was to their benefit _ we sold everything from hardware to homemade bread. And we installed a telephone for their use and a freezer for ice cream.

That bleak winter, we were visited by two Mormon friends, Mike and Vicky Ison. There in our cabin, with the winds howling outside, Vicky gave birth to a baby boy with a nurse serving as midwife. It was exhilarating to see another new life come into the world _ but I could not help feeling homesick, remembering Sunshine's birth at Pond Ridge.

Despite the freezing temperatures and snow, life in Montana did have it's funny moments.

Jeff, the youngest of the adopted children, never created any problems for us. If he got into trouble, it was usually because he had followed the lead of his older brother, John. Maybe Jeff was young enough that we were able to have a positive influence on him. God only knows.

The Mormon church we attended was about 30 miles away. John had developed a crush on a young girl at church and he decided to make sure we arrived early enough for him to talk to her. He convinced Jeff to help with his scheme.

The boys' regular chores before church was to haul water from the spring. To achieve their goal, the boys set the clock ahead an hour and slipped out of the house during the night and hauled the water, using trash cans on a cart pulled by their pony.

Looking back at the incident, we laugh but that Sunday, we were upset with our boys when we discovered we had arrived at church an hour ahead of schedule just so John could visit with the girl.

Our break with the Mormon church came after my final visit with two missionaries to a Mormon temple in Canada. I saw the same Mormon doctrine we had watched on the film in Washington, this time it was presented by performers prancing around on stage.

I again was disturbed seeing Adam portrayed as God. The young man playing the role of the devil was wearing a business suit with leopard skin socks pulled up over the pant cuffs.

The whole scene suddenly struck me as a force of deception. I looked around the temple and noticed a number of people sleeping through the program. I realized the irony was that we had been deceived, lulled into a sleep for years, thinking that we had been serving the Lord but we had played into the hands of a demonic cult.

That ended our relationship with the Mormons even though it was years later before the church officially excommunicated us.

As the winter turned into spring, we discovered our children were treated very coldly at the Amish school. As hard as they tried to become a part of the community, some of the Amish children would tease ours for being English.

Finally, we concluded the Amish had not realized we truly wanted to join their lifestyle. We weren't interested in joining their church. After the Mormon experience, we were not ready to join anything. We enjoyed their lifestyle and that puzzled them. Their invitation to take part in their school and their ways had been more of a courtesy to us _ they apparently had not considered it a long-term arrangement. We were invited to their church services in their homes a couple of times but this too appeared to be a courtesy.

The Amish said we couldn't continue in their school _ they feared the presence of our children would turn their school into a public facility. They apparently were concerned about another family they had allowed into the school for a couple of days. Their children used profanity and wrestled down the Amish girls.

The end result was the Amish church implemented a new rule prohibiting non-Amish from attending their school.

The most painful incident that grew out of our year in Montana was the severing of our relationship with John.

Mark, the young man from Kentucky who had played a key role in our joining the Mormons, followed our family to Montana. But to our shock, he no longer lived the All-American image. Mark's mail came to the store and I could not help noticing the predominant literature he received was magazines about firearms, human torture, and Adolph Hitler, the Nazi leader.

When we discovered this twist in Mark's personality, we forbid John from seeing him. We were not successful in helping John comprehend the change in Mark. Furthermore, this 14-year-old who dreamed of becoming a missionary like Mark, could not understand our leaving the Mormon church.

John began having emotional outbursts we could not explain or understand. Rage such as we had experienced with his older brother Alex. One day he threatened Vicky Ison, who along with her husband and four children was still with us in our cabin.

That was enough. Jerry contacted John's grandmother _ she agreed to take him. We bought a plane ticket and sent him back to Michigan. Jeff idolized his older brother and we feared John's influence on Jeff.

Years later, John was arrested for robbery and landed in prison. Then when he was nearing the end of his sentence, he walked away from a prison work detail. He was caught and to our horror, was lodged with more hardened criminals.

We fear for John's safety, his health, and most of all, his spiritual condition. He has become a lost sheep who has strayed from the flock but we still love and pray for him.

Looking back, we realize we gave up too quickly on John. God did not guarantee us success with every child who came into our care. We refuse to allow this painful episode to sidetrack us from helping others.

When the school year began that fall in Montana, we tried home schooling. However, when Becky, who was 7 by then, and the rest of the children would see their Amish friends walking by the store, they would cry. Plus, my teaching time was limited while I tried to operate the store, bake bread, and care for the family.

One day, when Jerry saw Becky burst into tears because her former Amish friends went by the store without waving to her, he broke. "That's enough. We're going back to Kentucky."

The children's faces turned to beaming smiles and they started jumping up and down, chanting "Hot rise biscuits and bluegrass fields!"

Life as a Mennonite

Back to the well-known blue grass fields of Kentucky. Back to Martha White's Hot Rise biscuits the children remembered from Pond Ridge!

Gone from Montana. Gone from the blizzards of winter and the dust storms of summer. Gone was the hunger of wanting to be accepted.

Welcomed with open arms indeed! Jacob Oberholtzer, minister of the Mennonite church, had arranged a rental house for us on South Fork Creek, about 20 miles from our former home at Pond Ridge on the Casey-Lincoln County line. The Mennonite women had cleaned the house for us and rounded up used furniture to start housekeeping in the heart of their community.

We had come to know Jacob and his wife, Mabel, from our earlier years in Kentucky. Jerry had been the van driver for the Mennonites when they needed to go to town for supplies or to special events like weddings in other states. Occasionally, Jerry had helped harvest their crops when they were short handed or the weather was threatening.

Once Jerry and I had taken Jacob and his family to Indiana for the wedding of one of his 17 children. Due to the huge crowd after the wedding, we took turns eating and Jacob listed our name to be called just like they would in a restaurant.

"Oberholtzer Vondriver," called a Mennonite to the group of wedding guests waiting outside. No one moved. "Oberholtzer Vondriver," he called again as everyone looked around for the family.

Jacob came out, heard who his Mennonite brother was calling, and then he came over to us, smiling.

"Jerry, Sandy ... it's your turn to eat." Instead of listing our names, Jacob had written down "van driver" by his name. And we heard him call it out as "Oberholtzer Vondriver." Vondriver was us!

We laughed about the incident as we moved into our new Kentucky home in October of 1979. Jerry began working with the Mennonites to learn their ways of simple farming. No tractors. Horses were our power. The work was hard but I could sense a new peace had come over my husband and our family.

The women helped me sew Mennonite bonnets and aprons for the girls. Even though we had not been Amish, I had taken to wearing Amish bonnets which are hard in front with a Dutch effect and draped on the neck. Mennonite bonnets are round in the back, shaped more like a traditional bonnet.

Adopting the Mennonite dress code, we also did away with our vehicles and lived without electricity, and telephones were forbidden.

A very simple life with plenty of hard work, a peaceful existence. Discovering a relationship between man, the earth and God. Rising in the morning and going to bed in the evening by the gentle glow of kerosene lanterns. I learned to trim wicks on the lanterns and use a gas iron.

As a Mennonite, I became more frugal. If you ran out of milk, you had to wait on the cow since you couldn't go to town. If there were any beets and peas left from supper, you ate them for breakfast rather than allowing them to waste. That took some adjustment, even to use stale bread to make bread pudding _ there was no such thing as waste in the Mennonite order.

And we learned to prepare ahead, like making noodles.

We used flour, water and eggs to make a batch of noodle dough. This would be run through a noodle machine like a wringer on an old-fashioned washing machine to make sheets of dough. This, in turn, was run through an attachment to create different sizes of noodles. We would lay the noodles on the bed to dry or hang them on the clothesline. The children got a kick out of watching the process _ a bedroom full of noodles!

But the children didn't just stand around watching. They were expected to do chores like they always had and work was a way of life in the Mennonite community.

Our children began attending the Mennonite school. Their school was the former school building we had constructed behind our home at Pond Ridge but had never used. The Mennonites had dismantled it and brought it to Casey and reassembled it for their own school.

The Mennonites didn't emphasize education. Their school went to the eighth grade and our children did the same. They learned by working _ sewing, cleaning house, feeding the animals. After chores, entertainment was reading a book, not television. The children loved volleyball and parlor games.

A Mennonite day goes from dawn to sunset. By

Jerry hooking up horse and Mennonite buggy.

keeping the children busy, there are less problems. Children feel sorry for themselves if they just sit around.

Young Mennonite girls are taught to care for babies. When a woman has a baby, a teen-age girl is sent to be her maid until she recuperates. This girl will clean the house, make supper, hoe the garden, and milk the cows if necessary. When they are older, they are allowed to travel to other states to help in similar situations. This gives them an opportunity to meet others and to fellowship.

At first, I was impressed with the simplicity and obedience of the Mennonite children. I later learned they could be real stinkers at times just like any children. The Mennonite children are under the discipline of their parents until they are 21. Parents march them out behind the woodshed if it's needed. But there is always lots of love with the discipline.

Church was somewhat different for us _ everyone in the Mennonite community attends _ no one stays at home. The men greeted each other with a "holy kiss" on the lips and the women greeted each other likewise.

Jerry helped build the new church _ floors so clean you could eat off them. Men and women sit on opposite sides of the church. But it is as common to see a man with a diaper bag over his shoulder and a small child on his hip as it is for his wife. Older children sit in a section with an elevated, slanted floor so they can have a full view of the singing table and the full bench of ministers and deacon.

The service is in German but Jacob did a portion in English for our benefit. No musical instruments. The songs were sung in German but I could recognize tunes like "Rock of Ages" and "Just as I Am." At times, worship was "dry" for us because we didn't understand German.

However, these were godly people and we believed their ways would keep our children from being exposed to the world. Within six months after returning to Kentucky, we were full-fledged Mennonites.

One day I was approached about serving as the midwife for the community. I told them I had been present for Sunshine's delivery at Pond Ridge and for Vicky Ison's baby in our Montana cabin in the dead of winter.

"That's good enough," they said.

The church collected $125 for my initial equipment and to pay for my training at a weekend seminar in Lexington. Joanna Wilson, a neighbor who had a car, went with me for the training and assisted during my first couple of years.

The seminar turned out to be in someone's home with hippies lounging on the floor using profane language. When we broke for lunch, we decided not to return.

Joanna sometimes drove me in her car but many of those early pre-natal checkups I did by horse and buggy. Jerry usually prepared the horse for me but there would be times when I would have to hitch it to the buggy myself.

That was a new experience for me, just like learning how to deliver a baby. I tried to use a heavy dose of common sense to go with the books that I studied about midwifery. My mother had never emphasized education _ she was thrilled if I slid by with D's on my report card.

As struggling new Mennonites, we couldn't afford paper towels to wash windows. Besides, we discovered that vinegar and water and the ink on old newspapers polished the windows and made them sparkle. By 1981, my sister Debbie had remarried and moved back to Kentucky. She sent me a bundle of old newspapers to use on my windows.

Becky and Jessica often amused themselves going through the old papers, looking at the pictures.

"Mommy, look at the pretty girl," Becky said, pointing to the picture of a little blonde haired girl. Taking the paper out of her hand, my eyes were riveted on the child's photo and the accompanying story.

The picture was of Elizabeth, an 11-year-old Downs Syndrome child, in need of an adoptive family. She was living at Bewley Center, a Methodist children's home in Tennessee. I explained to my girls the story said she was up for adoption. They became excited.

"Can we adopt her, Mommy?" Becky cried.

"Please, Mommy. She's so pretty," Jessica chimed in.

A calling from God

Elizabeth's picture reminded me of my brother, Pat who is environmentally handicapped. My mother always considered Pat retarded and didn't allow him to do anything for himself, not even changing his shirt which he was quite capable of doing. In reality, Pat was a slow learner, not retarded, and has since learned to care for himself and his wife.

Lord, You used that picture of Elizabeth and my memories of Pat to begin working on my heart again. Planting the seed with another child. But this child was mentally handicapped. Would we be able to care for her?

Looking at the date on the newspaper, I discovered it was already a couple of weeks old. And the article said Elizabeth's picture would be shown on Knoxville television in hopes of recruiting an adoptive family.

"Girls, this child has probably already been adopted. This is an old newspaper," I said.

"Mommy, please ..." Becky pleaded.

"Go ask your father."

I watched from the window as my two girls raced out the door and across the field, pigtails flying in the air, to where Jerry and his horses were plowing. No tractor _ we were still Mennonites.

I watched him take the newspaper from their hands, wipe his brow with a handkerchief, and then speak to the girls. I assumed he had said yes the way the girls started jumping up and down and then took off racing towards the house. Jerry went back to plowing, having told our girls it was up to their mother.

We talked. And prayed.

The more we talked and prayed, we could not see this child living her entire life in an institution. Expecting to be told Elizabeth was already taken, we went to a neighbor's house to use a phone, hoping to settle our two girls down more than anything else. To our surprise, despite the publicity, there had not been a single inquiry regarding Elizabeth.

Since we no longer had our van as Mennonites, we had to hire someone to take us to Tennessee to meet Elizabeth.

Elizabeth had been prepared for our visit. She walked in, looked at Jerry, and as he bent down to say "Hi," she patted his beard, took his straw hat out of his hand and placed it on her head, and said "Cowboy." She hugged me and felt my face, turned around and proceeded to walk away. The case worker said, "Liz, where are you going? These nice people drove three and a half hours to see you."

She said, "I'm going to pack my "cuit-case." I'm going home with Mommy and Daddy."

Through Elizabeth, we realized God was providing direction on how we were to serve Him. He wanted us to adopt children like Elizabeth who needed care, who needed love, who no one else wanted.

Elizabeth became a member of our family. As part of the paperwork involved in adopting her, Tennessee officials contacted Kentucky's social services office. Of course, having been a foster home already, we didn't have any trouble winning approval.

With our help, Elizabeth started reading "easy books" and performing simple chores. Today, she still takes great pride in drying the dishes, a chore she claims for her own after years of seeing many more brothers and sisters join our family.

Leaving the Mennonites

Elizabeth moved into our home _ by this time we were renting another house with 30 acres. We wanted to buy it when our property in Montana sold. We had rented it out when we left, but to our disappointment, the renter failed to pay.

This new location in Casey County was near a creek which became a raging river after a heavy rain. You had to cross a footbridge over the creek to reach the house. When it was hot, we bathed in the creek. Other times we used a basin.

When the owners decided not to sell, we were disappointed, but Jerry worked a deal with Ivan Zimmerman, a Mennonite neighbor, to purchase five acres of wooded land on his farm. He helped us arrange financing until the Montana property sold.

In the spring of 1982 we started cutting trees on our land and stacking the logs to dry for our new house.

But a battle was beginning to develop in the Mennonite church. Jacob, who felt his whole flock should be fed from the Word of God, had been delivering portions of his sermon in English for our benefit. This apparently was causing a division in the church as some of the members felt they should stick with only German services. We felt like we were a thorn in their sides _ we vowed never to rock the boat, so we got out.

We pulled up stakes and moved to Scottsville in western Kentucky where there was a Mennonite church that emphasized a "plainer life" even more so than our Mennonite church in Casey County.

We heard the Scottsville church did everything by horse and buggy. Sawed wood by hand rather than chainsaws. No cars. Period. And they didn't have a problem with English services.

But a void remained in our lives.

At the Scottsville school there was a strict teacher who would slap children on their wrists and knuckles over the most minor thing. Our children would come home sick and upset and Jerry would become frustrated over their unhappiness.

We were struggling financially _ the Scottsville church arranged for us to operate the pickle station for the community but money hadn't started coming in. Jerry was unable to find other work. We were thankful to receive donations of food from others but a spirit of unhappiness hovered over our family.

One day, a Mennonite from Mt. Herman, Ky. stopped by and told us of his church that had English speaking services. We visited a service and were impressed _ they had harmonized music that appealed to me. They also allowed black cars and electricity.

We decided to move to Mt. Herman, but Jerry could not find a house to rent. He came home in a state of depression such as I had never witnessed.

"I don't feel like living any more," Jerry said.

I finally lost my Polish temper.

"What good is all this trying to get back out of the world if we can't fit in? If our family is not happy, what good is it?"

Jerry was silent.

The following day he went to Casey County to visit, to try to get his head straight. He returned home to announce we were moving back to Casey _ our Mennonite neighbors had talked him into coming back for another try. The women were thrilled too _ they still needed me as a friend and as their midwife, and I needed them too.

The children jumped for joy.

The school house we had built on Pond Ridge became our temporary home in Casey County. The school year had ended and we lived there until our log home could be finished.

The logs had already been cut before we had left for Scottsville. Now that they had dried out _ Jerry began constructing our log home in earnest.

And we received a bit of good news. Just three days before the bank was to foreclose on our previous home in Montana, it sold. So that debt was off our back.

One night while our home was under construction, lightning struck Jacob's barn. It burned to the ground in the fire which followed. Nearly 100 Mennonites from Virginia and Scottsville came to join the local men for a "frolic" to help Jacob raise a new barn. Starting at sunrise, the men went to work while the women prepared food for them. It was amazing. By 3 p.m. the barn was under roof and the hay fields had been cut.

Since they had come all that way, a group of the men from Virginia came over that afternoon and helped place the logs on the second story of our house. It was amazing to watch the men carrying the logs _ if it were a poplar log, here would go two men carrying it, but if it were oak, it would take six!

By the end of June, 1982, we moved into our new, permanent Kentucky home on South Fork Ridge.

We were a family of eight _ Jeremy, Becky, Jeff, Jessica, Sunshine, Elizabeth, Jerry, and I.

During the next two years, we began taking in more handicapped children. With the special needs of many of these new children, we could not do without transportation and electricity. Jerry dropped out of the Mennonite church, and bought a truck to transport our children to the doctor, but I remained a member. A year later, he bought me a gas refrigerator and gas stove _ he said it was impractical to cook for so many children on a wood stove.

Some of the women in the church had encouraged me to acquire the gas stove. They contended if I had one, maybe the church would revise its rules and allow them to have one also.

All of the women wanted a gas stove, except for one apparently. The rules of the church required a unanimous vote. I received a visit from church leaders to inform me if I didn't give up the stove, I would be denied the right to communion the following day. It was the hardest decision I ever had to make. The Mennonite women were like real sisters to me. I was torn but I had to follow my husband.

Our official participation in the Mennonite church ended after nearly five years.

New beginnings

After our experience with the Mormons and our time in Montana, we felt we had to leave the "world" to shelter our children _ we wanted protection from being deceived again. With the Mennonites, we had left completely _ unfortunately, we had lost touch with the reality of life.

As Mennonites, I discovered we were restricted to care only for family and other church members.

The Mennonites are godly people and are among our strongest supporters today. I continue to serve as their midwife and we respect their way of life, but we found to get completely out of the world was not practical for our family.

One of the frequent sermons Jacob would preach was a simple question. He would say if you were ever confronted with a situation which you had doubts how to handle, simply ask yourself the question, "What would Jesus do?"

Lord, how many times have I asked that question since

I first heard it? It has served as a guide for me so many times.

Our son Jeff remained in the Mennonite order for some time, taking great pride in his hard work and keeping his buggy in top condition. When he joined the church, we later learned he sent $5 to Jack and Ethel Wright at the grocery store near our former home at Pond Ridge. It seems he had stolen a pencil one day in the store and he wanted to make things right with them.

As Jeff became interested in dating the Mennonite girls, he was frequently rejected because he was the "son of a Tucker." The girls' families feared Jeff would leave the church as his parents had. Quite an understandable fear. Broken hearted, he left the Mennonite church and later joined the Army.

After we left the Mennonite order, Joanna Wilson, our neighbor who was my first midwife assistant, brought over a battery operated tape player and some preaching tapes. I read the name of the preacher and said, "Jimmy Swaggart. I've never heard of him." But his powerful preaching fed our hungry souls and we drank every word while using a set of batteries in a day as we cross referenced the Scripture from his sermon tape with our Bible.

"That's my kind of preaching," Jerry said. "Just like Power in the Blood."

Two of the tapes were on healing and worship. I had always enjoyed music and it was comforting as we went through a spiritual healing process.

We had left the "world" in an attempt to protect our children but we discovered we could not isolate ourselves in a closet. We had to be a witness for Christ in the world. We still oppose public schools _ we believe in a Christian atmosphere where we can train our children in the Lord so they can be

The original log home on South Fork Ridge

witnesses in the world.

After hearing the tapes, we found a real conservative Bible-believing church in Somerset, Ky., about 30 miles from our home. Bro. Emmet Lanham and his wife, Betty, opened their arms to us, taking us in as a family. We cherish the spiritual journey that God allowed us to travel, making us stronger and closer to Him.

Last year, after Bro. Swaggart's public confession of his sin and the avalanche of national publicity, I couldn't believe hearing that other churches and ministers experienced similar falls. Even in Mennonite and Amish churches, although it is very rare among the plain people.

Of course, we were devastated by Bro. Swaggart's confession. But he asked for forgiveness. I'm reminded of the Scripture where Jesus said let the person without sin cast the first stone. We grew to love Bro. Swaggart as a Christian brother who has faults just like every other human being. Who are we not to forgive?

After all, what would Jesus do?

Home becomes ministry

Jerry was changing _ he was loving every minute of our service to the Lord as adoptive parents. Though it was a constant financial struggle, we knew we were doing what God wanted.

About a year after Elizabeth came into our home, we received a call from Tennessee. Another Downs Syndrome child, James, needed a home. Would we take him too?

Yes.

When Tennessee contacted Kentucky officials again, we heard from local social workers. If we were interested in handicapped children, why not take ones from Kentucky rather than another state? They also had a boy named James who needed a home. The boy was deaf.

Yes, again.

We agreed, except we first wanted James from Tennessee since we had already made the commitment. They, in turn, agreed. However, the deaf boy's foster mother apparently decided to adopt him at the last minute.

While waiting in the social services office one day, I thumbed through a book with pictures of children who were available for adoption. One caught my eye and stole my heart.

I was informed we wouldn't be able to get James, the deaf boy, after all. "How about Christopher then?" I asked, pointing to his picture in the book. A visit with Christopher was arranged and he became ours.

We renamed him Joshua and he now is commonly called "Butchie." His bright red hair and blue eyes are a beacon for the light of the Lord. In a short period of time, we ended up with three mentally handicapped children _ Elizabeth, James, and Butchie.

James was a real comedian with his zany cross-eyed smile. He would portray a TV weatherman, using a broom handle as a microphone. Or he would preach and sing, his hands uplifted to God. During a storm, our "apostle" James prays.

And Butchie, our little freckled face, redheaded Huckleberry Finn, captured our hearts even though he struggles to say "Ma."

Butchie was the victim of severe neglect and malnutrition as an infant. His mother, a soap opera addict, left him in his crib, didn't diaper him or provide proper nourishment. Rags were scattered like kitty litter in his crib. When state workers found him, he was literally a vegetable, his head hanging like a cantaloupe on a vine.

When he came into our home in the fall of 1983, he had undergone a couple years of therapy. He was crawling, smiling, and trying to balance himself on uncertain legs. Within another year, he was running, climbing steps, and jumping on the trampoline.

Billy carries George while Amy looks on.
(1985 Courier-Journal Photo by Bill Luster)

Then came Amy, age 10.

A Mennonite foster mother, Hannah Kulp, contacted us about adopting Amy, a microcephalic child (her skull too small for her brain). Our hearts were captured again by her long blonde braids, blue eyes and beautiful smile. She can neither chew her food nor talk and is prone to choking, but she understands what is said to her and is learning sign language.

The Budget, the Mennonite newspaper, was to again come into our lives. Faith Mission Home in Virginia had been reading Jerry's column in the Budget and contacted us about taking Rosie, a 22-year-old black girl. Rosie's retardation is from lead poisoning which came from eating paint when she was about two years old. Even though she functions on a five-year-old level, Rosie is our official greeter, barreling through the house at top speed to be first to offer a hug when visitors come to our home.

After visitors overcome Rosie's initial greeting _ she

can knock you down in her excitement to be friendly _ they will sometimes hear her say: "Rosie a bad girl. Spank."

She will sometimes pinch and hit and has to be guided to a chair to regain control. After about a half hour, she wants to be sorry for her behavior and is repentive to everyone, including visitors.

Once when Rosie was at Faith Mission, she became lost in the woods overnight. It was the guidance of the Lord that led a search party to her before harm came her way.

Rosie likes to carry around empty vitamin bottles or small toys. And one of her favorite people is George, a foster child from Kentucky who came to live with us in 1984 at age 14.

George has grown into a husky young man and is a big helper in carrying things or helping the workmen with construction. But when he arrived, this child with a limited IQ of 33 was self-abusive, pinching and biting himself, throwing tantrums and trying to hit others.

It took a lot of bruises on my arms, but with discipline and chores, George has settled down and become a big help around the house. His parents could not handle him _ today, a big treat for George is to occasionally visit his natural mother.

"Going to get you, George," Rosie laughs, down on all fours acting like a monkey. You have to laugh not only at Rosie but at George's reaction.

"No way, no way," smiles George, as he pretends he's going to run from Rosie.

One person George is afraid of and will run from if allowed is a doctor. He has a phobia about visiting a physician.

Once when Jerry was in the waiting room with George at the dentist's, George clasped both of his hands over his heart.

"Heart. Home."

Jerry ignored him. George tried another tactic.

Still holding his heart, and his face flushed from anxiety about being at the dentist's office, George said, "Scared. Pee."

George was allowed to go to the bathroom but he still had to see the dentist.

Billy was also 14 when he arrived. Although appearing normal, academically he was on a fourth grade level. Both of his parents are blind and could not cope with his disabilities. After being with us for nearly four years and trusting Christ while in our home, he left in the winter of 1987 to return to his parents.

And then came Donald, Patty, and Milton _ a trio from the same family. All three are blind, deaf, mentally and physically retarded having been born from a first-cousin relationship that resulted in seven children, all born with six fingers and six toes.

Donald, who is also self-abusive, was 11 when he came in the spring of 1985, weighing only about 23 pounds. This pixie of a fellow smiles as soon as he's touched and cuddled.

Patty was 8 when she arrived, weighing 32 pounds. She's our little Orphan Annie with her head full of dark curls.

Milton was born on Christmas Day 1982 and was two when he joined our family. Like his brother and sister, he was discovered in filthy, pitiful conditions, the victim of severe child neglect and abuse. They were in such filth that the social workers first thought Patty's hair was a rag tied on her head.

The mother apparently landed in prison on fraud charges. She allegedly had pawned the children's state supplied wheel chairs, misspent their SSI checks and then claimed one month's checks were lost. She was issued new checks and cashed them, receiving two months of pay. Since then, she has been released and is allegedly searching for her children.

At the same time, we also had a foster child who eventually became so disruptive we felt he was endangering the welfare of all the children. We had to let him go back to the state. For awhile, we also took in a half dozen or so teen-age girls who were runaways and needed temporary shelter. They drained our energy to care for the handicapped children and we eventually gave up our emergency shelter status.

It has always hurt to allow a child to leave but we have learned there are some children we are not equipped to handle. The welfare of the entire family unit is our top priority.

By Christmas 1984, we had started filing the necessary papers to incorporate ourselves as a ministry. We selected the name Galilean Home Ministries after an orphanage that we had heard operated in the 1950s at Corbin, Ky. Just as with adoptions, we were to learn it would take some time before our incorporation would be finalized and IRS tax-exempt status would be granted. The paperwork and red tape seemed to be mountainous.

Again we had to wait.

We wanted to be in a position to increase our ministry to include more unwanted children and others whose families were unable to care for them. Our home was remodeled to include three complete bathrooms, and a 30 by 34-foot addition had been added for a family room and a bedroom. We now had 11 bedrooms. The house had been wired for electricity; the original log home was still heated by wood and the rest by gas. We were thinking of possibly placing three or four bedrooms in the basement if needed.

Jerry and I have always believed the elderly are precious. As large as our family had become, something was missing _ and it became evident what it was. Our children did

Sunshine, who was born at Pond Ridge, is pictured at age 8. (1985 Courier-Journal Photo by Bill Luster)

not have a grandmother. So we did the most logical thing. If we can adopt children, why not adopt a granny? And so Frances Elmer from New York came to join our family.

Granny, who lived in a self-contained apartment attached to our home, was an avid reader. One day, she showed me a copy of Readers Digest.

"Here's another child you need to adopt."

Our lives were never to be the same.

A celebrity child

Weldon Jackson Jr. found a home in our hearts and as a result, our ministry was to change forever.

Looking at Weldon Jackson Tucker today, it is difficult to believe this child was once given up to die, and if he were to live, he would be nothing more than a vegetable. And looking at our ministry in 1985 when we had 14 children at home, who would have believed that more than 60 would ramble about our home only four years later. Certainly not Jerry and I, Lord. You were about to take our ministry on a journey that would surpass our wildest dreams.

I met Weldon for the first time in the bleak days of February, 1985, in Texas. The first day I saw him, he was busy rubbing his bowel movement into his hair. I was able to look beyond that and see a child who with lots of love, could become normal in our home.

Based on the story I had read in the *Readers Digest*

which Granny Elmer had shown me, it was obvious that Weldon's success so far had been due to the love he had found at Alice Tutor's Nursing Home in Waco, Texas. The elderly residents had taken Weldon into their hearts like so many grandfathers.

Just like Elizabeth, I had expected countless inquiries about Weldon. But there were few. Lord, once again You had planned for us to adopt this child.

Weldon is legally blind and deaf. Because of his impaired hearing and poor motor skills, he walks in a gait resembling a drunken stagger. He loves to be held and cuddled and is making dramatic progress in learning sign language. Now nearly 10 years old, he is the unofficial greeter for visitors to our home, approaching each new face with arms outstretched for a loving hug as he snuggles close. He still makes a chirping sound _ it's his way of letting you know he wants to be held.

This is quite a different sight from when I first encountered Weldon. His nose was constantly running, food would come back through his nostrils due to enlarged tonsils, and his hair was more like a shag rug. They thought he had chronic lung disease from his wheezy breathing, but it turned out he was allergic to cigarette smoke _ many of the men at the nursing home smoked.

Weldon was born out of wedlock seven weeks premature in Korea, the son of a black American soldier and a South Korean girl. This Amerasian child had been born with multiple birth defects _ chronic respiratory condition, cardiopulmonary arrest and seizures, and an undeveloped espohagus.

The father discovered Weldon's birth certificate had been ripped up and the child had been pushed in the corner of the hospital to die. But the father refused to abandon his son

_ he talked a fellow soldier who was being transferred to Hawaii into helping him. The father stole the child out of the hospital and his buddy slipped the tiny infant under his coat and smuggled him out of the country.

Once in Hawaii, he took Weldon to the Army hospital where doctors performed open heart surgery. Later, when the father was transferred back to America and assigned to Ft. Hood, Texas, he took Weldon with him to another Army hospital. The child underwent operations to implant feeding tubes in his stomach. Doctors still gave little hope of survival.

In November 1980, Alice Tutor agreed to take Weldon into her nursing home until his father was discharged from the military. She questioned whether Weldon, who was then 10 months old, would disturb the residents. Most of her residents had served in the armed forces. She was told that Weldon had little chance of living, and at best, he would be a vegetable.

When he was discharged, Weldon's father disappeared, never formally establishing paternity rights. In effect, Weldon became a child without a home and a country.

The nursing home hired private detectives to locate Weldon's father. He was found and he signed over custody rights in late 1983, which opened the legal doors to grant Weldon citizenship. To win citizenship, it had to be proven Weldon had an American father.

The nursing home residents became Weldon's family, helping to care for him, once even watching him around the clock as he battled pneumonia. As he grew, doctors confirmed he was neither totally blind nor deaf. His vision impairment could not be corrected with glasses but his hearing could be improved with a hearing aid.

Weldon's story broke in *Parade Magazine* in 1983, and later in *Readers Digest* with the title "What This Boy Needs Is Love."

A scandal erupted when a retarded resident at the nursing home was accused of abusing Weldon. In January 1985, Texas officials removed Weldon from the nursing home and placed him in the care of a foster family. The state of Texas began looking for a permanent home for this child and the story hit the national media wires.

In February, Texas authorities agreed to allow Weldon to come to our home but several weeks elapsed before he arrived. While we were going through all the paperwork, we kept in touch with Weldon. We wanted him to know that we loved him and wanted him to be a part of our family.

His arrival was delayed once when Alice Tutor questioned the adoption. But her questions were finally resolved and Weldon was flown to Kentucky to join our family.

I had a Mickey Mouse doll for Weldon that said "Weldon" on the back and "I am an American Citizen" on the front.

Weldon became our "golden boy" because of his copper toned skin coloring and all the publicity. He has also become known as the "boy nobody wanted" and "the boy without a country."

When he was removed from the cigarette smoke, much of the wheezing stopped. After we had his tonsils taken out, he was able to swallow his food and, in turn, began to grow into a healthy young boy.

For us, it was not only a time of a growing family but with this "celebrity child," we found ourselves the focus of the national media. Weldon's story had attracted their attention, but in the process of him finding an adoptive family, the media discovered what was an even bigger story in their eyes _ a family willing to take in not only a handicapped child but one that had already adopted several. In the spring of 1985, our family stood at 14 _ eight of our children were handicapped.

Jessica gives Weldon a bath.
(1985 Courier-Journal Photo by Bill Luster)

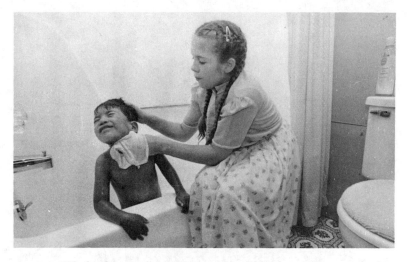

We had been interviewed by the press before, but this was an entirely different world _ there were TV cameras and lights, microphones, reporters firing questions over and over. It had only been a short time earlier that we had left the quiet life of the Mennonites _ now we were thrust into a beehive of publicity.

Readers Digest, Parade, People, the *National Enquirer, Newsweek, USA Today,* television network interviews by ABC's "Good Morning America," and several TV programs on Christian cables were to follow.

And there was a movie offer. Lew Hunter came to our home and lived with us while he roughed out an idea for a script. Despite the notoriety of our story, it never sold _ it appeared too "religious" for a secular TV audience.

But that's okay _ we weren't in it for the publicity. But the media attention was an opportunity to share our faith in Christ and let people know handicapped children could be loved and could love in return.

137

Tommy finds a family

"Mom, I want Tommy's tape recorder."

I had noticed James had gone outside sometime earlier. It was early spring, still cool enough for him to need a jacket. When I walked out on our front porch to call him, I noticed him returning down the lane toward home.

He walked up to me, gave me a big hug, and smiled. Then he told me he wanted Tommy's tape recorder.

"James, where have you been?"

"I went to talk to Tommy," James said. I could feel a lump forming in my throat. "Tommy said I could have his tape recorder."

Tommy, one of the most precious children God ever created in His image, had died earlier on Valentine's Day. He and James were both Downs Syndrome children and had hit it off as best of friends.

Here stood James telling me Tommy had said he could

138

have his tape recorder. I gave James a hug, wiping tears, and then excused myself.

Tommy, 19, arrived in July of 1985 following the publicity blitz surrounding our adoption of Weldon. This Downs Syndrome child had partial use of only one lung and required lung treatments three times daily.

Tommy, who had been available for adoption since he was two days old, had lived in three different foster homes before being placed in a nursing home at 18. We finally convinced the state we could care for him.

Jerry visited Tommy in Louisville _ he was a big University of Louisville sports fan, always dressed in red U of L sportswear. We could not bring him immediately into our home because the regulations said we could only have one foster child over 18.

At the time, Rosie's adoption had not been finalized and we also had another older girl, Denise, a loving mentally retarded child. We arranged for our friends Max and Jean Dunlap to assume foster care of Denise.

While waiting for Rosie's adoption to be completed, Jerry visited Tommy each week and Tommy would count off the weeks until he could home with him.

"I go home with you in five more visits," smiled Tommy as he would color in one of the books Jerry had brought him. He would become so excited about finally having a his own permanent family.

The big day came.

The Louisville social worker loaded Tommy and his oxygen tanks into her van and headed to Liberty. But other state officials had failed to tell her that they had changed their minds because Rosie's adoption had not been finalized at the last minute. They called the state police and had the van stopped under the excuse that sufficient oxygen was not on board for the trip.

"You said I could go," sobbed Tommy. The social worker cried and cried with this broken-hearted child over the bureaucratic foul-up. When we learned what happened, Jerry burned the phone lines off to Frankfort contending that Tommy had a constitutional right to a family. They finally relented and agreed to allow him to come on to our home without Rosie's adoption being completed.

Tommy was so happy as he was adopted as a brother by the other children. Jeremy took a special interest in him and would ride in the ambulance with him when we had to take Tommy to the hospital for medical treatment. A nurse usually came a couple of times a week to check on him but we were able to make sure he got his oxygen treatments.

We would tease him about being a U of L fan. Since we lived near Lexington, most of the folks we encountered were University of Kentucky fans. It was such a joy to see him laugh as he always insisted U of L had the winning team.

Tommy was unable to make it to our annual outing at Thanksgiving for the children to serve food to the needy at the Salvation Army in Lexington. He was in the hospital and once we had served the last person, Jerry took the children to the hospital to visit him.

"I love you Mom," Tommy would always say as he would reach out for my arm as I walked by. And I loved him like a son.

Tommy's death came on Valentine's Day in 1986, within a week of his adoption being finalized. Tommy Bluebaum Tucker was buried in the little church cemetery near our home.

And I gave James his tape recorder.

A happy Tommy in 1985.

Sandy and James, 1988. (Caring People Magazine Photo)

The doors open

During the winter of 1985-86, we finally opened our own Christian school in our basement. By then, Kentucky's laws allowed for such a private school _ we hung the biggest copy of the Ten Commandments we could find! We arranged for a sign language teacher _ Ina Price _ to help us begin special classes.

The school was easily filled with the children we already had plus those who followed from the media coverage that came with Weldon's arrival.

Rebekah, 11, came in the spring of 1986. Her adoptive parents, Tom and Judy Osterhaus from North Carolina, had been praying for a loving home in which to place her. We formally adopted Rebekah the following year.

Christine Hunt from Faith Mission Home in Virginia, and Donna McCray from Lexington, both came in the fall of 1986. They have mental handicaps but were trained to help with the housekeeping and to assist with the children. Donna has since rejoined her father and enjoys helping smaller children in Bible School and Sunday School.

Christine, who is now 28, had lived at Faith Mission since she was eight years old. The staff is composed of volunteers who spend about six months and then move on. We learned Christine would become attached to a worker and then they would leave. She had developed violent mood swings which built up until she would lash out.

The first few months Christine was with us, she disliked Becky, confusing her as a volunteer worker. One morning we awoke to hear Becky screaming.

I found Christine hitting Becky with a curtain rod. I grabbed a wooden salad spoon with a long thin handle and bent Christine over my knee and spanked her. I told her to never hit Becky or anyone else again.

"Sorry Mom."

"Christine, don't ever touch the children again. You're going to be here forever."

With that, I saw Christine's whole countenance change.

"Me don't want to be Christine Hunt any more. Me want to be Christine Tucker," she said as we hugged. Christine had truly become a member of our family.

If anything, she overworks herself, helping to bathe the babies and assisting with housecleaning. She'll clean up a baby with the dirtiest diaper that ever existed and will never complain about it. Sometimes I have to stop her in her tracks and force her to slow down.

Roger, 14, came in the fall of 1986, a severe cerebral palsy child. During his stay with us, he accepted Christ and was filled with the Holy Spirit. Always smiling, Roger was never able to overcome being separated from his foster parents who had cared for him from the age of 4 until he arrived in our

143

home. In the winter of 1987, he moved to be closer to them.

Joining us in the winter of 1986 was tiny Ramsey _ 16 months old and 16 pounds of sweetness with blond hair and blue eyes. He is severely afflicted with cerebral palsy and has a history of being tossed back and forth to eight different homes. His mother kept his normal twin sister; she loves him but is unable to care for his special needs.

Ramsey's body muscles often draw up creating severe pain. His crib is equipped with a special water mattress to ease his discomfort. His cries bring immediate attention from whoever is the closest to him at the time, whether it be a staff associate or one of the older children. Even though he is now 4, his small size, baby blond hair, and sparkling blue eyes remind you of an infant.

Ramsey was Donna McCray's "boy" when she was with us. She would hold and rock him for hours, changing his diaper and feeding him whenever needed. And if a photographer ever took a picture of Ramsey, she always asked for a copy of "her baby."

As 1986 neared an end, we received our IRS tax exemption _ almost two years from the time we began the process. The Christian Appalachian Project, Joe and Dr. Mary Hardesty, and Maurine McGuire in memory of Faye Congleton Hobbs, helped us financially to construct an addition now known as the "babies' room" where most of our bedfast children stay. With all these extra children following Weldon's arrival, by the end of each day I feel like a mountain climber who has reached the top. By then of course, Lord, You were moving us toward expanding our hearts to take in children from Haiti.

Reaching out

My God doesn't have any geographical boundaries.

That's the lesson I learned as we were led to bringing surgically correctable children from Haiti to America. And that thought has been burned into my heart time and again as children from Haiti, Honduras, Guatemala, Afghanistan, and Brazil have come into our home.

Children from across the United States had come to us but I never dreamed God meant for us to go beyond our borders. I was to discover God knew our weakness _ children _ and when I saw these beautiful faces, I knew He had unwanted children in other countries for us to love too.

In early 1986, Jerry and Charlene Leach, a Lexington family who supports our ministry, heard Rosemary Platel speak at a church about the need for Americans to be involved in caring for children from her Haitian homeland. Rosemary operated two orphanages in this poverty-stricken country but said she was not equipped to care for handicapped children. The impression I had later was that Rosemary was in the "adoption business" for financial gain, but her plea was used to speak to my heart and I needed to go see for myself.

And when I saw the children, I knew our ministry was to be involved. We were to take a new step in faith and reach out to more unwanted children.

On my first two trips, I was joined by Mary Lou Weldy, our friend at Christian Life Ministries in Liberty. The first was a fact-finding mission and the second was to deliver $900 for passports and medical fees to prepare six handicapped children to come to America for surgery.

During that first visit, Mary Lou and I were greeted at the airport by Haitian children playing drums. It was the smell of urine that greeted us when we arrived at Rose Mary's orphanage, the Voice of the Poor.

Some of the children sang for us but many were on beds without sheets, some laying in their own diarrhea. The poverty and pain were even worse when we visited a clinic in a 100-year-old sugar mill. Residents had walked for miles to carry their children to a doctor.

Then, we visited the hospital _ I saw immense pain, underfed, dirty children imprisoned in ancient cribs, some desperately ill, some profoundly retarded. Many had been tied in their beds so they wouldn't have to be fooled with; others were covered in mosquito nets to keep away the flies. But more flies were under the net filling the mouth of a dying child.

Children flooded the streets. Taking baths and playing in sewer water. Others grabbing chicken bones from the garbage at a restaurant where we ate. And children were begging everywhere.

On the second visit, we stayed at a motel _ we felt as if we had died and gone to heaven. Running water and a flushable toilet! One night, however, I discovered the biggest roach I had ever seen. Mary Lou laughed in stitches as I chased the varmint around the room in my nightgown, my hair falling down, with sandal in hand.

I had remembered the begging children from my first trip. This time I brought a roll of new shiny pennies, ink pens, some Granola bars, and when all those were gone, I gave away dates from a box I had stuffed into my big black purse at the last minute before leaving home. The children treasured those as much as the ones who got shiny pennies.

We were trying to get three children cleared for medical help _ Jean and Elenue, two cousins with deformed legs whom we met at World Vision's orphanage, and Baby Marie, a six month old who needed an operation for water on the brain, was brought to us by her mother. Jean looked at the trip as a big adventure, while Elenue remained frightened. Through tears one night, she sang "What a Friend We Have In Jesus" in her native Creole. We were crying by the time she finished.

While in Haiti, we had met a delegation from a church in Goshen, Indiana. where Mary Lou's husband, Dale, once attended. Among the group was Terry Smith _ a young man God was to touch later to volunteer his carpentry skills numerous times to help us with building projects.

The church group was instrumental in locating officials we needed to talk to, but everywhere we went, the political leaders wanted money under the table to secure the necessary passports, physicals for the children and their visas. We were down to our last day before we were to head back to America and I was tired of "come back tomorrows."

That night I cried out, "God, this is Your project. If You want this baby to go with us on that plane, then You have to take it from here as we've done all we can. Our time is up."

At 10 the next morning, immigration officials told me to come back in 10 days. I burst into tears, explaining our plane was to leave at 4:30 p.m. and we wanted these children to go with us.

"What am I going to do with a crying woman?" the official asked. "Come back at 11 a.m."

God softened his heart. We had the necessary physicals completed for the children and returned. It was discovered we did not have a birth certificate for Baby Marie. Rosemary stepped forward, told the official the child was in her custody at her orphanage and she had the power to sign the permission slip.

I had never dreamed Rosemary could sign the papers. Noticing the smiles on our faces, the immigration official said, "Go catch that plane."

The big adventure was about to begin. Off to the plane we went, Mary Lou carrying Baby Marie while I was helping Elenue and Jean, who were using brooms as crutches. As we headed to the plane, Jean's hat blew off. I watched in amazement as he went chasing it, running with one leg, and then reaching out, snatched it with the broom.

Hurrying to the plane, I realized the clerk at the airport had short-changed me a dollar for insurance required on Elenue at the last minute. I started to turn back and ask for my dollar but Mary Lou convinced me that with all we had gone through, I was better off to not risk more questions _ let them have the dollar.

Arriving in Miami, we were questioned for another hour and a half. Immigration officials wanted to make sure everything was in order _ by this time I was tired and frustrated. Looking back, I can understand the American officials had the children's best interests at heart.

We passed the final red tape hurdle and off to the hills

of Kentucky we went, practically running out of the airport.

Baby Marie had surgery immediately. This six-month-old child had water on the brain and needed a shunt implant. A nearby medical clinic had offered to donate their services for the operation but changed their mind. We turned to the University of Kentucky Medical Center for the operation and issued a plea to help pay the $7,000 bill.

In October 1986, I returned Baby Marie to her mother. This lady had given birth to her only child at age 42. Lord, how I remember the joy on that mother's face. She cuddled her baby with one arm and lifted the other up in praise to You, shouting over and over "Merci, Jesus." Her thanks to You brought tears to my eyes.

In September of 1988, Baby Marie returned to our home for corrective surgery. She was now two and a half years old and her shunt implant was malfunctioning. This baby, with her saucer eyes and chubby cheeks, has since undergone the surgery and returned to her loving Christian mother.

Elenue and Jean, cousins who were 13 and 10 respectively when they arrived in the fall of 1986, have since had their deformed right legs amputated and have been fitted with prosthetics.

That fall we took our children, along with the new ones from Haiti, to Washington, D.C. Our congressman, Harold Rogers of Somerset, arranged for the children to meet then vice president, George Bush. As the television cameras rolled and cameras clicked away, Jean sang "Jesus Loves the Little Children of the World" in his native Creole for Mr. Bush. Jean's eyes turned to big saucers when the vice president joined him singing in French.

Red tape continued to plague us. World Vision had failed to get a waiver signed by Jean and Elenue's parents and the orphanage director quit in the middle of the process. Their surgery was delayed until the summer of 1987. The paper-work was eventually accepted by Dr. Maynard Stetten and Kosair's Hospital in Louisville donated their services for the operations.

That fall, our children presented their musical program at a church in Atlanta, Georgia. After the service, we were approached by a woman who was deeply moved by the children and their testimony. She said her son was a prosthetics' manufacturer and she would see if he could help.

Before we arrived home from the long journey, her son, Jan Wooten, had telephoned. Jerry called back to hear him say, "My mother told me your story. The children will be provided the prosthetics they need."

Thank You, Lord. Jean and Elenue received their new legs just before Christmas. They both proudly showed them off to the children and to the press as they walked on them for the first time.

Both children are bright, friendly and enthusiastic about their new lives. Jean learned to ride a bike with only one leg while Elenue prefers to keep both feet on the ground.

Jean has a tendency to take off his artificial limb when he's playing softball, contending it slows him down too much. Elenue, who wants to learn how to drive, sleeps with her leg on. During a big snowfall, Elenue had to have help getting back into the house _ the artificial limb had frozen while sledding in the snow and she couldn't straighten it out.

But these children have received more than artificial limbs. Elenue is among the many children who have come to trust Jesus as their personal Savior during their time in our home.

The Galilean Home children with Vice President George Bush and Congressman Harold Rogers.

Jean uses a crutch in getting used to his new artificial leg. (1988 Danville Kentucky Advocate Photo by Sallie Bright)

"I wait."

Our next Haitian child was Effie.

I met Effie when I returned Baby Marie to her mother in the fall of 1986. She was in an orphanage run by a Florida-based relief group, World Harvest for Christ.

Effie, 6, who was born with congenitally deformed legs and feet, had been abandoned four years before. Records indicated Effie's parents had eight other children in a two-room hut. They were subsistence gardeners who were unable to care for her.

Madeline Hundy, a missionary with World Harvest for Christ New Life Center Children's Home, and her husband Nigel, traveled four hours by boat and another eight over rocky roads to bring Effie to their orphanage. Questions arose about her birthdate and delayed the paperwork.

The mother made the long journey herself to give officials Effie's birthdate. Still, the paperwork could not be completed in time to take Effie back to America with me on that mission trip.

I told Effie we would do everything we could to bring her to America to have an operation so she could walk.

"I wait," she said. My tears flowed.

Within 10 days, Effie was in America, brought by Cindy Rogers, a nurse from Georgia who works with World Harvest. Effie, who had never worn shoes or felt the cold, arrived in November 1986. On the plane trip, Cindy said Effie kept saying "Effie Kontann" meaning "Effie Happy." And over and over she said "mache," meaning "walk."

Effie had been treated for tuberculosis and malnutrition. Orphanage officials believed she suffered a dislocated hip at birth. When she came to our home, it was thought she needed hip and foot surgery and possibly braces to walk.

However, Shriners Hospital could find no reason for Effie not to walk. By the summer of 1987, baffled doctors said Effie only needed therapy and lots of tender loving care. And that she got at our home along with many prayers that one day she would walk. Shortly before Christmas, she mastered the art of balancing herself and took her first tentative steps.

By the spring of 1988 Effie was walking after eight years of crawling, evidenced by her calloused knees. Promised a new baby doll, this mentally sharp child started taking her first steps. And she is gaining her balance, even though she is somewhat tipsy at times. Only God knows what this child's medical problems are but her infectious smile is contagious around our home.

Also, during that trip, I saw two babies abandoned at General Hospital, both with cleft palates, hardly weighing more than four pounds. Those tiny infants tore at my heart. The doctor reluctantly agreed to allow me to have them if I could complete the paperwork before I was scheduled to leave

153

the country.

I did. But when I went to the doctor for the children, he could only stare at me as I reached out the necessary paperwork to him. He remained silent.

"Doctor, you said I could have those two babies if I completed the paperwork," I said. "I have and I've come for the babies."

He continued to stare at me, refusing to take the visas out of my hand. Finally, he turned and left the room with no comment.

I felt his nurse's hand on my shoulder.

"Mrs. Tucker. I'm sorry. The doctor never dreamed you could obtain the papers for the children. He sold them yesterday to the voo-doo doctors for $1 apiece."

I stood in absolute horror. Defenseless babies sacrificed for a dollar!

During the trip, a Christian radio station had heard about my visit and asked me to come for an interview. As I came back down the mountain from their station, the Jeep radio was playing a song called "Bring That Child To Me" that had been dedicated to me.

Tears flowed as I thought of the two little children who had been sacrificed to the devil. I could not conceive of a society that allowed human sacrifices like this. Those babies, even though they had critical medical problems, could have touched the hearts of some childless mother.

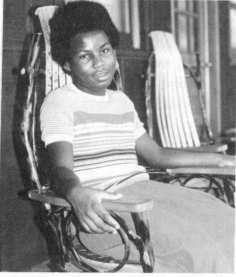

Effie greets Becky with a kiss. (1986 Courier-Journal Photo by Pam Spaulding) At left is Rose, who became a Christian during her stay at the Galilean Home.

A blooming Rose

My fourth mission trip to Haiti was to take medical supplies and clothing to children. This time, I met Rose, a 12-year-old child born with both female and male organs. As she had grown, she was developing more male tendencies and her alcoholic father had thrown her out on the streets to live. Her mother, a Christian, could not deal with her.

Rose landed in a children's prison and detention center with more than 350 other children, many of them throw-away children rejected by their families and peers. In Port-au-Prince, a city of a million, 5,000 children are abandoned every year. The children's prison director, Paula Thybulle, had asked me to help get Rose out.

On the trip to America in the summer of 1987, Rose's eyes grew as big as quarters. She ate her first luxury meal on the plane _ eating her roll first, followed by the dessert, the salad, and finally the meat.

Rose became the 32nd child in our home. I think that's right, Lord.

The first week in our home, Rose did fine but then she regressed. We saw a child who without a doubt was possessed by demonic forces. She would try to eat paper, gravel, rocks, plastic, aluminum foil, soap, and shampoo. She would get a stare in her eyes, begin pulling her hair, biting her arm or trying to choke herself.

One Sunday, about 40 visitors were at our home for a tour. Earlier, Rose had been trying to rip off her clothes. Jerry took her to another room to try to restrain her while I conducted the tour. Finally becoming exhausted, Rose fell asleep on the floor.

Without my knowledge, a group of men in the delegation had slipped away and discovered the room where Jerry and Rose were. These precious men of God laid hands on her and prayed that she would be freed. Jerry said the prayer was short but full of power and when they were finished, one of the brothers said, "It is done!"

Rose had slept through the prayer but when she awoke, she started crying and hugging us, saying she loved us. Praise the Lord, this child had been freed _ her former behavior did not return.

It took months to get Rose's medical visa. In the fall of 1987, she finally underwent surgery to reconstruct her female organs. Louisville gynecologist Dr. Clinton Cook and Norton Hospital did the operation free of charge.

Rose asked if she could stay long enough to see her first snowfall. Lord, You knew what You were doing. Later that fall, Rose accepted You into her heart.

By the time Rose returned to her Christian mother in the spring of 1988 _ after building her first snowman _ she said she wanted to become a missionary, possibly to India. Eleven months earlier she had arrived controlled by the devil; now she was leaving a Christian.

Freedom for Berto

By this time we had become experts at red tape. During
my visit to pick up Rose in Haiti, I had encountered a young
man named Berto, who cried to go back to America. I could
not erase that tearful face and plea from my mind. More than
a year later, Berto joined our family in September of 1988.

Big tears flowed down his face when I saw him that
first time in Haiti. The director of the children's prison, Centre
D'Accenuil et de Re-education, had told him to go away, that
I was there for someone else. Berto was a street child in the
worst slum in Port-au-Prince. He never knew his father; his
mother died when he was four and he shared a dirt floor shack
with five or six relatives.

A volunteer with a Christian youth group came to
know him on successive mission trips. When he married, the
newlyweds decided to adopt Berto, but it didn't work out.
Berto tried to bite a teacher, attempted to slash a girl with a

razor blade, and would scream in fits of hysteria.

His emotional outbursts apparently began when he learned his new adopted mother was going to have a baby. Berto's adoptive family sedated him and sent him back to Haiti where he was returned to the children's prison.

Once again, Congressman Harold Rogers came to our aid, and was helpful in obtaining a new visa for Berto. It took months because his American family had to relinquish their parental rights to him.

Sure, we have encountered problems with Berto. Once, coming back from a singing engagement, he tried to jump out the door of our van. But he has adjusted and has learned our commitment to him is for life, that we love him and he won't be returning to Haiti.

Berto is a real businessman. He doubles rewards he gets from making good grades. We give every child in our school 25 cents for a perfect score and 10 cents for passing (above 80). Berto buys things and resells them for a profit. This past year, he completed the most school work in his class.

Emanuella and Sandy arrived from Haiti in October of 1988. It took a humanitarian parole to get these two children out. Congressman Rogers appealed to the Secretary of State to achieve this. Some American officials had rejected the earlier requests, saying America didn't need these children _ they were going to die anyway.

Sandy is gaining weight but still appears frail. She smiles with her bright eyes as they follow every move you take in caring for her. You can sense she knows she is loved.

Emanuella, once near starvation, is now a chubby cheeked little imp who races about in her walker. Renamed Destiny, she is being adopted by Alta Martin, our school principal.

Sunshine, at left, welcomes Sandy with Baby Marie from Haiti, Marlon from Honduras, and Berto, also of Haiti.

Alta Martin, principal of the Galilean Christian Academy, picks up Destiny, a child from Haiti she is adopting. Looking on is Abigail Fowler.

More American children

Within the next couple of years, God would lead us to more children from Third World countries but before that happened, He would send more to our home from throughout the United States.

Chris, a dark-haired moppet who came in the winter of 1986, had a vocabulary of about 50 words. He recently turned 9 years old and late this summer he moved to Faith Mission Home to receive training for the educable mentally handicapped.

He was followed in 1987 by Lance, who was 7. He came from St. Joseph, Missouri. for cerebral palsy treatment and care. His father, Mike Brown, is an associate pastor of a church in South Lyons, Michigan.

Robbie and Ernie arrived in the fall of 1987 after more than 21 months of red tape. Their foster parents in Syracuse, New York learned of our home through a television program.

Robert and Lilian Cormack had been foster parents for 40 years, caring for more than 120 children during that time frame, and were now in deteriorating health. Unable to care for the boys any longer, they asked us to take them.

Robert died of a heart attack a short time after the boys left. Lilian, who has diabetes and failing eyesight, did not want to see the boys end up in an institution.

Ernie, 14, is not as advanced as Robbie, 13, who doesn't speak except with his eyes. The boys require constant diaper changes and attention _ neither appear to feel pain nor express emotion. When they are in bed, we have to restrain them to prevent them from falling.

Once a staff worker was walking by Robbie's bed and noticed he had a tear on his cheek but his face mirrored no pain or any sign of discomfort. Since he cannot speak, there was not any obvious way of determining the problem. After taking him to a doctor, it was discovered he had a severe ear infection.

Dawn, a 21-year-old mentally retarded woman, was with us for a season in the fall of 1987. She later returned to her home in northern Indiana.

Anthony, 9, was also with us for a few months. Society had labeled this hyperactive child with an Attention Deficit Disorder. His rejection simply fed more rejection. He is now with our friends, Jake and Sharon Shaible who have a ministry for troubled boys. Anthony is making dramatic progress in their home and continues to attend our school.

Thelma is another special lady. She was 35 with the mental age of a 6-month-old when she came the winter of 1987. She receives lots of special attention and is deeply loved and accepted by the other children. Her brother, John Systma, and his wife, Judy, had cared for her for many years before asking us to assume her daily care. Thelma busies herself by clapping large spoons together, closely examining her feet, or simply looking out the window in the family room, watching the tree branches with their pretty green leaves bouncing in the air.

And the young lady who has stolen the hearts of every member of the family is Baby Alicia, better known as "Sissy." She was born Jan. 5, 1988, and arrived from Baton Rouge a few days after our 25tth wedding anniversary. She has spina bifida, club feet and hydrocephalas. Later, she will undergo surgery to straighten her hip sockets and feet.

She has won the hearts of everyone _ especially Jerry. In our crowded quarters, Jerry insists that her baby bed remain in our bedroom.

Candy, 4, and Mara, 5, were also with us for about a year. The adopted mother of these two Mexican girls was having eye surgery and asked us to care for them during her recuperation.

Lynnie, 17, and Sharon, 14, were also with us for a few months last year while their foster mother was adjusting to married life. Sharon joined our girls in singing at churches, stealing hearts everywhere she went.

Melissa, Kristi, and Brad are three adopted children who arrived last summer in time to participate in our Christian school because of learning disabilities. They have excelled.

Zachary, 6, and Bradley, 7, are brothers by adoption through a Jewish family in Florida. They came here last summer after difficulties arose in bonding with their new family. Bradley allegedly was asthmatic, allergic to milk, and threw severe tantrums while at home but did not experience those kinds of problems here.

Bradley has returned to his adoptive family but Zachary chose to stay. He enjoys being with the other children, especially wrestling with those from the Third World countries.

We also have nine children living here who are members

of staff residents. Eli is the son of Joy Calcine, one of our teachers, and Caleb, Inca, and Keterah, are the children of Olivia Calcine, our laundress. Joshua and Dan are the sons of Sammy Murphy and our house parents for the boys' dormitory, Tony and Brenda Luce, have three children: Antonia, Amanda, and Rex.

Sandy with Sissy, who has stolen the hearts of everyone at Galilean Home. (1988 Caring People Magazine Photo)

A special lady

"Sandy, what are you all talking about?"

Mam was in her usual place at the end of our huge family and dining room to be close to the children. A child was in Mam's lap explaining that her baby doll was sick. At her feet were several little children playing house. She had been Grandma for them, talking in a pretend squeaky voice.

She had overheard my conservation with a visitor and had broken in with a question. I had been talking about abortion and how the presidential candidates were battling each other over the issue.

When I explained to this 99-year-old-woman about abortion, her usual deep smiling face turned to a look of horror. She couldn't believe such insanity.

"Why that's murder!" she screamed.

Jerry's grandmother, Jane Frances Tucker, had come to our home from Michigan in the summer of 1987. To

everyone, she was "Mam."

Mam, who as a child had been cared for by a black servant, registered so she could vote for George Bush who had voiced his opposition to abortion.

I once asked Mam if the noise from all our children bothered her.

"No, Sandy. The noise of children is music to my ears," Mam said. "Children are the sound of life."

Ask her if she were feeling all right, this witty woman would fire back, "I'm half left" or "I can walk better than the day I was born."

Mam often talked about wanting to live to be a 100. But just before Christmas last year, she died at the age of 99.

This special lady, who discovered that the horror of abortion is taking place in our country, did live to be a 100, argues her son Frank, Jerry's father. He contends if you count the time Mam was in her mother's womb, she was 100 when she died.

I believe that's the way Mam would look at it.

Financial burdens

In 1988 and continuing into this year, we have experienced an unprecedented growth in our ministry, a growth that leaves us standing in awe at what God can do, and frankly, a little frightened at the scope of it and the money it takes to keep it going.

When we adopted Elizabeth, our first handicapped child, it was certainly an act of love. But as more and more came our way, we realized God had been preparing us all these years for a ministry to care for and love His little lambs, many of them unwanted by others.

We called our service to the Lord the Galilean Home Ministries. It took a couple of years to obtain our non-profit corporation and IRS tax-exemption status. But we didn't let that stop us from going ahead and accepting children in need of love.

It was also a hassle to obtain our Mentally Retarded

167

Developmentally Delayed (MRDD) license from the state, but this group home status enables us to keep some of the handicapped foster children past 18 years of age. We ended our participation in the state foster care program last year and began accepting children from private sources.

When we lived at Pond Ridge, our bill at Wright's Grocery for food and supplies averaged $400 a month. The winter after Weldon came in 1985, costs had risen to $3,500, including the staff we added to help care for our growing family. By the time we received our tax exemption in the winter of 1986, we were at $16,000 a month.

Today, with more than 60 children and a staff of 40, our annual budget is nearing three quarters of a million dollars. Of the $60,000 needed monthly, only about $10,000 comes from federal Supplemental Social Insurance payments. We must rely upon caring individuals and churches to provide the balance.

We continue to press on in faith.

In 1988, we realized a number of building projects which had been in the dreaming stage for years. A physical therapy room was started with a grant from WHAS Crusade for Children. A laundry room with two bedrooms upstairs was begun with the help of a grant from Christian Appalachian Project, and McDonald's Charities gave us $5,000 to start a building that houses a boys' dormitory on the first floor and our Galilean Christian Academy above.

Our water bill was averaging $5,000 a year because we had to have water hauled to our cistern. In late 1987, Tom Isaac and David Clark, who were to later become members of our financial advisory committee, paid for a waterline to be extended to our home from Ivan Zimmerman's spring. With a steady supply of water, we were able to build the badly needed laundry.

The Galilean Home, November, 1989: At left, physical therapy room and women's staff quarters; original log home is behind trees; next is babies' room and girls' dormitory; wash house and bedrooms; school and boys' dorm.

We then installed more clothes washers and dryers. Ora and Helena Davis took on finishing a girls' dormitory above the babies' room and plumbing the laundry facility. It is a full-time job for our laundress to keep up.

Our biggest joy is our new school. Christian education has always been one of our major concerns _ we have seen what can happen to children in public schools. We haven't cut any corners on our school, hiring eight teachers and we'll be adding more to handle our growing number of children plus those from the community who want out of public schools.

Our school has come a long way from the basement in the winter of 1985-86. Today, the children are learning to use computers and their schoolwork is from the Accelerated Christian Education curriculum.

There are plenty of educational field trips and physical education classes to go along with the daily chapel services.

Our principal, Alta Martin, came from Sheldon, Wisconsin in 1985 when she was 19 to volunteer her summer to teach Weldon sign language. She had heard about Weldon and our home from a woman who had seen us on television and realized she had met me when we lived in Montana. Alta returned in 1987 to become a full-time teacher and is now the principal of our new school.

Exposure through the media and in church presentations has brought more children and additional financial support.

But, financially, we have our ups and downs. For example, in February of 1988, we suffered a $10,000 shortage of funds we needed for that month. Our secretary at that time felt led by the Holy Spirit to write our supporters, asking for a simple $1 donation from each. An unbelievable $40,000 was generated and was a tremendous blessing at the time.

However, our debts have continued to mount. Late last year, we formed an advisory panel to assist with our finances. These Christian businessmen have been helping us bring some of our expenses under control, getting materials donated to complete our building projects, and coming up with ideas on fund raising. And they have been special prayer partners for our ministry.

The advisory committee is composed of Chuck Cotton, chairman; Skip Adams, Dave Clark, Guy Colson, John Hendershot, Tom Isaac, and Bob Myers.

God has always pulled us through each crisis we have encountered, financial or otherwise. We're trying to listen for His voice in how to handle our finances. Sometimes we either fail to listen or misunderstand but I know our hearts are in the right place and He will help work everything out for His glory.

A Caring Award

In December 1988, we accepted the national Caring Award in the name of Jesus Christ. We were always caring people. The only difference is that before we accepted Jesus Christ as our personal Savior, we only cared about ourselves. Our life is now dedicated to caring for others, especially those who cannot give back anything in return.

Bill Halamandaris, director of the Caring Institute of the Foundation for Hospice and Home Care, said the process was initiated in 1985, a concept that was designed to reinforce people who help others, an award dedicated to service. The members of the institute said they had discovered not enough recognition and attention was given to those who really make a difference in society.

More than 20,000 letters went out across the country seeking nominations. Our congressman, Harold Rogers, nominated us. Of the nominations received over a three-year period, we were among the 12 award recipients.

Halamandaris said he was stunned when he met all of our children and saw our home. He had discovered from working on a major film documentary about chronically ill children that there is much red tape involved and many of these children have a lifetime disability. He couldn't imagine anything any more real. When he said people have difficulty in attending to the needs of one child, I told them they don't have enough children. He said we dealt with the same bureaucracy but we multiplied it by the dozens. Our faith and courage in the Lord sees us through the red tape _ many of the children had illnesses or problems or limitations but they were so obviously happy.

The institute's goal through the Caring Award is to help the recipients gain more attention, and in turn, gain more support. Also to create an identity of "caring, reflections of the human heart," to encourage others to do something for future generations.

The institute used our picture with Mara and Candy on the cover of their new CARING PEOPLE magazine. In the article, Congressman Rogers said: "The Tuckers set an example of Christian love and compassion that all of us should emulate."

I don't know about people emulating us but if this award helps others begin caring for unwanted children, then praise the Lord!

Jeff helps Ishmail of Afghanistan with his computer lesson at the Galilean Christian Academy.

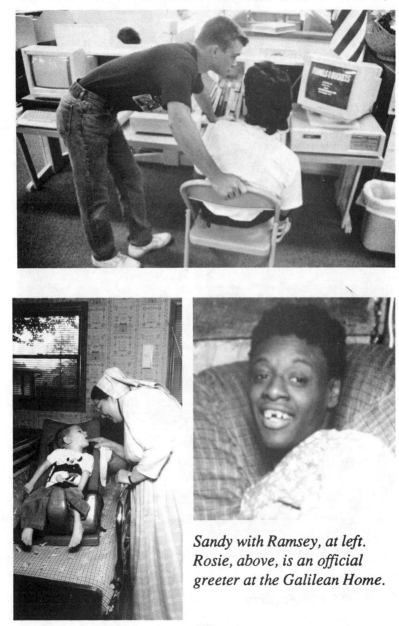

Sandy with Ramsey, at left. Rosie, above, is an official greeter at the Galilean Home.

Candy gives Andrea Fowler some pointers in cleaning the table. (1988 Kentucky Advocate Photo by Sallie Bright)

Boys' dorm director Tony Luce with Zachery.

Becky tells Weldon "I love you" in sign language as she prepares to leave for Bible college.

More Third World children

In the spring of 1988, we found ourselves launched into a massive effort that brought children to us from other Third World countries like Guatemala and Honduras. Two of our most recent additions have been two boys wounded by the Russians in their war against Afghanistan.

The majority of these children have been referred to us by Healing the Children of Spokane, Washington.

Alberto Valentine Olivia, 13, arrived from Guatemala sitting on a skateboard. He was afflicted with polio at a young age and was given braces by a missionary to help him walk. However, Valentine's father took them away, saying the child could make more money begging without them. He acquired a skateboard and was to spend the next few years begging on the streets of Guatemala. When Valentine first arrived, Jerry discovered a razor blade taped to the bottom of his skateboard. He explained he had it there for self-defense but Jerry ended that _ Valentine has learned he doesn't need such weapons in our home.

Valentine's legs were put into a full cast to help him stand and is now undergoing extensive physical therapy to strengthen his hips so he can walk with braces.

Oscar arrived with Valentine from Guatemala. The smile of this four-year-old steals your heart and he has learned to use English especially when he wants a cookie. His legs are still in casts where doctors have actually operated to turn his little frog legs around and straighten them. Even now he is beginning to take tentative steps with the aid of a special walker on wheels.

I cried with joy when I found him one day standing in his crib on his legs in casts. Once his treatment is completed, Oscar will be returning to his Christian mother.

Dora, 16, arrived last fall, about to lose her foot through infection acquired after an attempted club foot surgery in Guatemala. In the process of examining her, the doctors discovered she had a 12-inch tumor on her spine. Dr. Bill Schwank of Bowling Green removed the tumor thread by thread using a laser beam. The surgery required more than 13 hours but it was completely successful. And the doctors have only had to perform a partial amputation of her foot. The tumor was the cause of the club feet.

Marlon was our first child from Honduras. Jerry discovered this eight-year-old last year while he was in that country helping build a church as a missionary project. Marlon's withered polio-stricken leg will need therapy and a brace so he can walk without a crutch.

Christian, 11, came from Guatemala last September suffering from infected deterioration of his leg since birth.

Luki, a 10-year-old spina bifida victim from Guatemala, joined our family before Christmas. She bears the scars

176

of rape and abuse over a six-month imprisonment by Army soldiers at their camp. A priest found her and another girl and arranged for Luki to come to America. She needs extensive recorrective surgery because of loss of bowel and bladder control due to the abuse.

Luki walks with a limp and has a sweet smile. When she first arrived, she did fine until she went to our church camp on a Sunday outing. Margaret was with her when she became hysterical and detected the child thought she was back in an Army camp. Margaret gave Luki a doll and lots of hugs and she calmed down, going off finally to play with the other children.

Oscar, 10, from Honduras, has congential abnormalities of a crippling nature. His brother and sister have the same condition and will be coming to our home also.

He arrived with Jose, 7, at the first of the year. Jose, who has become known as Yankee Joe Gringo, has severe club feet. He greeted me at the airport by pinching and biting me.

Brenda, 16, was only with us a few days in March. This Guatemalan teen-ager has been given about 18 months to live. But, God, we know You can perform miracles. Ninety percent of the arteries from her heart to her brain are plastic and only half of those are functioning.

Christina, a 15-year-old Indian girl, and her badly burned son Roberto, arrived in March from Guatemala. The child's face was burned off, including his eyelids, nose and lips. Weighing only six and a half pounds upon arrival here, he has since gained 10 pounds in three months and has undergone the initial plastic surgery at Shriners burn unit in Cincinnati.

Omar is a photographer's dream. This tiny boy born with one leg eight inches shorter than the other is being followed by newspaper and television crews during his stay in

America.

Another arrival from Guatemala in March this year was Marvin, 7. He will have surgery on a leg which was broken more than a year ago and never fixed. The ball was broken off the top of his thigh bone. No medical treatment or repair was available and infection (osteomyelitis) set in, resulting in excruciating pain.

Marvin's devoted father carried him on his back for the three-hour walk up a mountain from the clinic where we were screening children during a trip to Guatemala in January. Susan Fowler, who has joined our ministry as a grant writer, accompanied me on that trip.

Ofilio, a Guatemalan boy, nearly 18, tried to jump a train in Bowling Green, Kentucky earlier this year. He had been working as a migrant worker since he was 13. Jumping trains was common to him but this time he paid a terrible price, slipping and losing both legs.

"You be my American ma ma?" he asked when I went to see him at Lexington's Shriners Hospital. Lord, how could I say no.

But just before Mother's Day you sent me nine more children.

The first two were from Afghanistan. Both Umar, 13, and Mohammad Ismail, 14, are here for leg injuries suffered in the war with Russia.

Umar witnessed his cousin's instant death when he stepped on a land mine as they were walking across a field. In a bombing by a helicopter, Ismail said he saw his parents and brother killed.

It is a new experience for us to have Muslims in our home. Despite their Pushtu language, we have been able to communicate. At first, they thought we were Russians based on our appearance. Through an interpreter, Abdule Gafur, in

178

Lexington, we were able to calm their fears.

Seven more children from Guatemala were among those who arrived before Mother's Day.

Abel Orlando, nine, lost his arms when he grabbed an electric wire while climbing a tree. However, he has learned to write with his toes and has captured the hearts of the other children.

Incarcion Monray, 18, has been robbed of his vision from a accidental chemical spraying of fruit trees on Christmas Day 1987. Infection set in and took his vision. He has had a cornea transplant and regained partial eyesight.

Others include Nancy, an apparently deaf three-year-old, who clucks like a chicken, bites, spits and pinches others to get attention; Jennifer, 12, has no hip socket in one leg; Claudia, seven, her legs practically swivel completely around because she does not have hip sockets; Carlos, 10, here for hip surgery, is to be adopted by a Washington family; and Sandy, an eight-year-old Indian girl who doesn't talk much but seems to be responding quickly to our home. It was said she never talked at home.

Children from around the world: Reinaldo, left, from Brazil; Valentine and Incarcion from Guatemala, and Umar from Afghanistan.

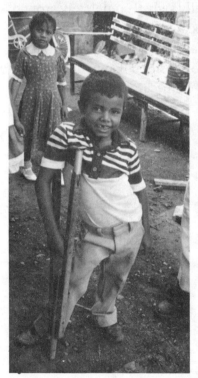

Donnie Swaggart holds Roberto from Guatemala. At left is Marlon of Honduras.

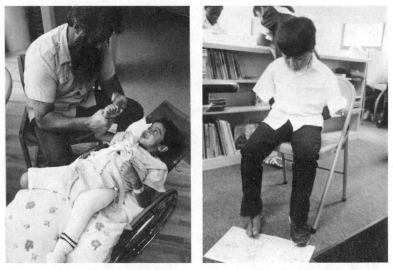

Jerry with Omar of Guatemala, top left. Abel, also of Guatemala, who lost his arms in an accident, uses his toes to write. Below from left, are Rebekah, George (background), and from Haiti, Baby Marie, Effie, and Elenue.

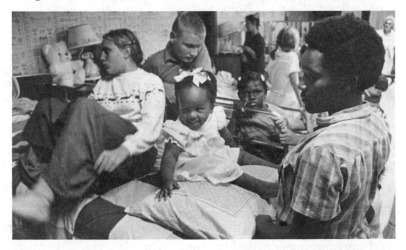

On the firing line

"What's your name?"

"Wiener."

"His real name is Oscar."

The church congregation bursts into laughter. Tiny Oscar, his little legs in casts, his eyes bright with excitement, lays his little head over on my shoulder and hugs me. He's been teased so long by the children and staff, I really believe he thinks his name is "wiener."

Oscar is not the only show stopper when we present a church program. Sissy, when she tires of playing on the platform, will reach for me to hold her while we're singing. Without fail, she'll grab the microphone and pull it over to her and start singing her "daddy" song. "Da - da - da- ..." Jerry, of course, loves it _ he'll be holding her before the program ends.

We've had the opportunity to travel across the country sharing our testimony in word and song. I only wish more handicapped children could go along for everyone to meet but I know our staff is able to handle any problems that arise. Despite the tremendous amount of time it takes to get 40 to 50 children ready for a trip and the long drives back home, we enjoy it.

Time and again, we've seen hearts touched by these little children.

Abel, our little Guatemalan boy who lost his arms when he grabbed a power line while climbing a tree, singing "Jesus Loves Me" in Spanish. Jean singing it in his native Creole. Or Mara, one of our two little Mexican girls, helping with a song about child abuse, "Dear Mr. Jesus."

Then there's James raising his hands in praise to the Lord _ in his mind, he's preaching about Jesus. Once when I introduced Elizabeth, our first mentally handicapped child, she pulled the microphone away from me and said she wanted to sing "Jesus Loves Me." And she did. Tears flooded that service.

We've seen hearts touched and souls saved by the testimony of these children. Not only did God use children to lead us to His son Jesus Christ, He's using these little lambs to help others find Christ today!

In addition to seeing the lost accept Christ, our church presentations help us raise finances to support this ministry. Finances earlier this year became a nightmare hanging over our heads.

Month after month, our financial contributions have not been what we need to care for more than 60 children. We had been falling short about $20,000 a month for several months. These deficits, plus our previous bills from earlier years, has pushed our debts past the $100,000 mark. Of that amount, more than a third is for unsecured debts _ from food bills to utilities.

Our financial advisory committee has tried a number of fund-raising ideas to get the money coming in on a regular basis but so far, we're still running behind, far behind.

At a meeting earlier this summer, recommendations were tossed around the table to bring our financial house in order; otherwise, fears were being expressed that our ministry would be facing bankruptcy. The proposals were unbelievable.

Let all the children go who are not adopted. Find other homes for them.

Close down your Christian school. Send the children back to public schools.

Slash expenses.

Get rid of some vehicles. And staff.

Then it was Jerry's turn to respond.

"Will each of you take five of my children that aren't adopted?" he asked. "Will you change your lifestyles to make sure these children have a home?"

No comment. Finally, one spoke.

"This is wrong. We can only offer advice and support them. We can't tell Jerry and Sandy what to do."

The meeting was interrupted by a telephone call.

"This is Sandy. Tell Jerry I've been arrested."

Waiting

She looks older than 18, this girl in handcuffs with stringy blonde hair, her face aged by experiences I don't want to think about. Apparently she's a juvenile. Why else would she be in this courtroom?

As she waits for the judge, a child advocate volunteer questions how she's being treated. Satisfied, he asks who's watching her infant daughter. Babies having babies!

Across from me is a father, his face clouded with anguish. His teen-age daughter is beside him, absorbing the surroundings. What is her crime, I wonder.

Her face lights up as another handcuffed young woman enters the room. It must be her sister. She and her father stand to greet her but the jailer tells them to sit. They cannot visit before the hearing, but I notice the father communicating with eyes filled with pain. Does he fear for the future of the child by him; will she too end up in trouble like her older sister?

They sit down to wait.

And I'm waiting too.

Waiting for weeks now to see what happens to a young child sent to us, we believe by the Lord. A young child whose story we believe about being abused, abandoned, and neglected over the years. Her family has arrived _ they look like they would be at home on the front row at church.

State troopers served me with a warrant. I had refused to return a child who maintained she was abused. They said the warrant allowed me to avoid being arrested if I would hand over the child.

Off to jail I went _ without bond. I would wait the rest of my life out behind bars if necessary before I would voluntarily allow a child to go back into a situation believed to be abusive. Our attorney protested, claiming I was being treated like a serial murder suspect. The bond conditions were changed, allowing our attorney's wife to go to the courthouse and post a property bond for me.

The child was placed in a home in another city and we have been allowed to visit twice a week. After weeks of preparation, our attorneys still warn we may lose the child through a technicality in the law. But Jerry and I have trusted God to intervene in her behalf. After we prayed earlier this morning, we told each other we had peace about the outcome but sensed confusion as to how it would be achieved. Now, we must wait.

Waiting. Our whole lives have been filled with waiting.

I remember waiting in a courthouse to finalize Jeremy's adoption. Before that, nearly seven years of waiting, trying to have a baby and then pursuing adoption, only to be turned down by agency after agency.

As we adopted children in Michigan, our waiting was

186

interrupted twice by million-to-one chances of having my own biological children, but then came Becky and Jessica.

And the Lord waited on us all those years. We wandered around pursuing our selfish desires for children. Then He used children to get our attention, to help lead us to Him after we heard His Word preached, after we learned of the "PAR-ER IN THE BLOOD."

Followed by more waiting. For Sunshine's birth one midnight on Pond Ridge. For the blizzard of bad experiences to end in Montana. For resolving the struggle whether to keep our children "out of the world" by remaining in the Mennonite order.

Waiting to find out if Elizabeth had been adopted. Whether someone else had opened their hearts to this Downs Syndrome child. Waiting for the Lord's confirmation that He was calling us to a ministry of helping handicapped children.

Then followed by months, even years, of waiting for non-profit status from the Internal Revenue Service, and to be licensed as a group home by the state. An obstacle we had to overcome with the IRS was to prove we were a ministry, not just a large family trying to get tax breaks.

With each adoption, came long months of waiting to finalize them. Waiting on bureaucracy. Red tape. Public officials.

As the family and ministry grew, we learned to wait upon God's people for financial support. Once, Jerry said we had gone beyond our limits and declined to take two children. Funds stopped coming in. For days. When he resumed the adoption process, a $5,000 check arrived in the mail.

In the last couple of months, our financial crisis has eased as supporters have responded to our plea for help. We did not feel led by God to let any of our children go or to close our Christian school. Instead, we have "put more water in the soup" as Jerry describes tightening up the budget. We believe the Lord has honored our efforts as we have waited upon Him to bring in the necessary funds.

I remember waiting in Haiti. Red tape in America is overwhelming, but it's exhausting in Third World countries. Once, I just leaned against a building in Haiti and waited for authorities to arrive to sign visas. And I waited against the wall. For hours.

Waiting in doctors' offices is more comfortable. But as more and more children have come from Third World countries for surgery, the waiting has increased.

And as a mother, I have waited to hear from my grown children.

A call from the family soldier, Jeff in Germany.

Or from Rochelle and Luella, former victims of drug abuse, who have got their lives back on track.

A letter from John in prison.

A call from Renee. She has become a loving, faithful mother with two children who encounter more discipline than we ever dreamed of dishing out to Renee.

Laurie. We've lost contact with her, but somewhere out there, she must know in her heart we love her.

And I wait to hear from children who have left recently. Like Mara and Candy, our two little Mexican girls who have returned to their family. Or Bradley, back in Florida with his adoptive mother. And Carlos, from Guatemala, who has been adopted by a Washington family.

With the waiting all these years, has come patience and hard work. No eight-hour days, when you have 60 children, a staff of 40, and constant attacks by satan upon this ministry.

Like the one we are undergoing with this child.

The courtroom is nearly empty now. Because of the

large number of witnesses, the judge apparently has decided to hear our case last. Jerry is pacing. Our attorneys are huddled in a corner. I do not like the expressions of doubt I see on their faces.

Our case is called.

Not all the witnesses can fit into the judge's chambers. The bailiff apologizes, but assures everyone they will have an opportunity to speak if the judge calls.

The judge does not summon them though _ the main characters are present. This time the waiting is brief.

The decision. Those the child claims have abused her will not get custody today. Nor will we. The case will be returned to the local court and the child will be placed in a foster home until a final verdict is reached.

Victory for those who wait upon the Lord!

Outside the courtroom, Jerry lifts his hands in praise and shouts "Hallelujah!"

The smiling child hugs other girls with us. They give her quickly handwritten notes of encouragement.

An attorney who has been helping us stops our delegation. We committed this case and the child to the Lord, he says. Let's give Him the praise.

And we do. A prayer of thanks. Right there on the sidewalk.

Our other attorneys are stunned by the victory. But they point out there is much yet to be done to gain permanent custody. They say we can expect to wait months before a final verdict.

We've learned to wait upon the Lord. Before, we've waited for months, even years, for children. This is no exception.

A *lost sheep is found*

Will that be our son?

A bell rang each time an inmate entered the visitation room. Lowell Bartels, our Christian friend we had met at the national Caring Award presentation last year, had picked Jerry and I up earlier in the afternoon at the airport. Our plane was late and by the time we collected our luggage, visitation had already begun. Was John somewhere behind those walls thinking we weren't coming after all these years?

The young man walking through the door was not John. He went over to a nearby table and greeted a young woman with a Bible. They hugged and kissed. As I heard the bell ring again, I turned back to see the door opening.

Will that be our son?

It has been six years since we had last seen John _ we were working on the original part of our log cabin on South Fork Ridge. John had recently been released from prison after serving time for auto theft. I was heartbroken after John left us in Montana and then later got into trouble with the law in Nebraska.

No, the prisoner coming through the door was not John. But as quickly as the door closed, the bell rang again, announcing someone else was about to enter the room, always under the watchful eyes of the guards. My eyes remained fixed on the door as I sensed Jerry leaning forward in his chair.

Will that be our son?

John had broken into a liquor store, without a gun, and was captured and ended up here at Deerlodge Prison in Montana. Since his crime was non-violent, and he had earned the confidence of prison officials, he eventually became a trusty which allowed him more freedom than most other prisoners. But then as he neared parole, he escaped in the back of a laundry truck with the help of another inmate. He was quickly apprehended and was placed under tighter security with more hardened criminals.

This young man, who had once enjoyed riding horses at Pond Ridge and stuffing himself with fried chicken on Sunday picnics, had fallen into the drug world within the prison.

In December, 1988, we, along with 11 others, were presented with the Caring Award at a banquet in Washington, D.C. Jerry and I were introduced to fellow recipients, among them Lowell Bartels of Montana. A close friendship followed. We learned God had fit yet another piece into His marvelous puzzle.

Lowell, an operator of a chain of restaurants, shared with us about his ministry to help the handicapped and visiting in prisons. We shared the sorrow of a son in a Montana prison.

Lowell began visiting John and years of silence were broken. John began communicating with us by writing letters home. Then he hit us up for money. At first we sent him money but then stopped doing so when we realized it apparently was going for drugs. He broke off contact with us.

Lowell believed in order to reach John and to open communications again, Jerry and I needed to personally visit him. John had seen media accounts about my trips to Haiti and our bringing Third World children to Casey County for medical care. One day he threw in Lowell's face that if we could go to Haiti, why couldn't we come to Montana?

John was the lost sheep from the fold. We decided to leave our flock of children _ who were safe in the care of our loving staff _ and went to find our son, our lost sheep. Lowell made the arrangements with the prison and we postponed a church program for the weekend visit. Lowell warned us that in his previous visits John had always been untidy in his appearance, unpressed clothing and hair flowing down his back. We went expecting the worst but we had come to find our son, to let him know we loved him.

Will that be our son?

The tension was gripping me as I heard the bell ring again. The young man's face broke into a wide grin as he spotted us. Was that John? He appeared so small, so frail _ but oh, so clean. His clothes were neatly pressed and his hair was not long!

We hugged.

And kissed.

And laughed.

And cried.

During the next three days, for as many hours as we were allowed, we visited John. We saw our son turn from a figidity ball of nervous energy on the first visit to a relaxed young man laughing as we played a game of Scrabble. We stayed with Lowell and his family when visitation was over

Sandy and Jerry with John, October, 1989.

and the excitement from finding our son was contagious as we shared about John until the early hours of the morning.

John was astounded when he learned we hadn't combined the visit with a church appearance in the area or a television program interview. We had traveled hundreds of miles with the sole purpose of seeing him, to let our son know he was loved.

We asked about the drugs.

"It's a way of passing a day. I never smoked or did dope until I got into prison. The high comes from the adrenalin rush you get from doing whatever you have to do to get the drugs in here. The drugs just help you pass a day. Without it, a day in prison becomes like a year."

I couldn't believe I was hearing our son say this. By the grace of God _ that phrase was sprinkled throughout Lowell's conversation _ we would get help for him.

Jerry tried to share the Lord with him.

"Dad, I don't want to hear about that religion stuff."

"Son, I had to try. It's my duty and obligation to God."

"I know. You wouldn't be Dad if you didn't."

John contended those who claimed to be Christians in prison were hypocrites, carrying their Bibles for protection. I pointed to the young man with the woman we had seen with a Bible.

"No, he's straight."

On our last visit, the young man came over to our table and introduced himself.

"I'm Barry. John told me last night you were his parents. Would you like to share our morning devotions with us?" nodding to his girl friend.

"Sure!"

We prayed together and read Scripture. Barry had trusted Christ in prison, and later had become friends with Kerry, a former prison nurse. He had been instrumental in helping her regain custody of her two children who were also visiting him.

We discovered Barry also had led a number of men to Christ while an inmate. He said he asked God to send him someone each day to share the gospel with. He volunteered to help John and be his friend behind bars. Barry said man had sentenced him to more than 100 years behind bars but Jesus had set him free.

I praise God that He can still reach down and touch lives of even those behind prison walls and set their souls free.

John was full of questions about the other children. Jeremy, Jeff, Sunshine, Jessica, Becky. When he learned Becky was nearly 19 and in Bible college and had never had a date, he said he couldn't believe it.

"John, if Becky were with us here today, she would probably be up, moving around witnessing about Christ to other men in this room," Jerry said.

"No way," John said. "I wouldn't let her. No man in

this room is going to take advantage of my little sister."

By the time our final visit came, John was talking of making a sincere effort to make parole. We offered him a private room in the boys' dormitory and a job so he could earn enough money to get his feet on the ground.

But the ball was in his court, Jerry reminded him.

"Dad, I'm going to try."

One of the most beautiful experiences for me was to see Jerry and our son together. For the first time, I believe they discovered that despite the previous conflicts when John was in our home, they truly had a father-son relationship.

Lowell had asked John about his hair.

"I got it cut for Dad," he said.

We're now back in Casey County.

Back to the daily routine of being mother and father to more than five dozen children. And the calls keep coming, wanting to know if we can take another child.

"Yes," I say, trusting God to provide the finances and the strength to move forward with The Galilean Home.

We have faith.

And hope.

And room for one more.

The phone rings again.

Will that be our son, John?

TO BE CONTINUED

EPILOGUE
Where love abounds
NOVEMBER, 1989

My wife, Carol, and I have had the pleasure of helping Jerry and Sandy with the writing of their book, *Faith, Hope, and Room for one more*. Let me share some closing thoughts with you.

Jerry and Sandy are real people.

Sometimes you have to pinch yourself to make sure you're not dreaming when you see their love for Jesus Christ lived out by loving these 'lil lambs, as Sandy calls the dozens of children at the Galilean Home. You question how Jerry and Sandy survive the daily trials they encounter in protecting an abused child or keeping their ministry financially afloat. They admit to making mistakes along the way, but they don't try to hide them. If you attempt to love a child, it can never be considered a failure.

Jerry and Sandy obviously have given up their private lives to be God's servants in shepherding abused and handicapped children from around the world. Has it been worth it?

Ask Jeff.

Jeff, one of the seven children Jerry and Sandy adopted before their conversion to Christ at that little county church, attributes his walk with the Lord today to the influence of his adoptive family. He recently returned from overseas after serving his country for two years in the Army. He turned to God's Word and gospel music as outlets for his spare time rather than partying with other soldiers. As a result, Jeff has grown in the Lord, a young man who also has observed growth at home.

*Sandy and Jerry Tucker
(1988 Caring People Magazine Photo)*

"Mom and Dad are able to love five dozen children as easily as when there were only a few of us," Jeff told me. "Dad has mellowed. When I was at home, if he noticed a baby needed changing, he would have called for one of my sisters. Today, he would change the diaper himself if he couldn't quickly find someone."

"I strive to be the best," Jeff said. "That's what Mom and Dad would want and that's what I want. To be the best for the Lord at whatever I do."

Ask Elenue.

Within the last month she returned to Haiti, a young teen-ager who came to America to be fitted for an artificial leg. But while at the Galilean Home, she also learned to read, and most important, she trusted Jesus Christ as her Lord and Saviour. Imagine the impact this young woman can have for the cause of Christ in her native homeland.

Ask the dozen bedfast children.

In their hearts and minds, they have to know they are cared for and loved. I can't conceive of them smiling at you with their eyes like they do if they were confined to an institution.

Ask Marlon.

Jerry met this crippled boy in Honduras while helping build a church. Jerry introduced himself to Marlon's parents at a church service, telling them that one of the ministries of the Galilean Home was to help children needing medical care. Marlon's parents responded in tears that they had prayed for years asking God to provide their child a way to America for help. Wouldn't you love to be present when they see Marlon come home able to walk without the aid of crutches?

Ask the child found abandoned on the street.

Ask the boy who was sexually abused by his father.

Or if he were alive, you could ask Tommy.

Can you sense Tommy's joy the few months he lived at the Galilean Home? This Downs Syndrome child had been available for adoption since he was two days old. At 18, Jerry and Sandy discovered Tommy in a nursing home and successfully waged an effort to provide him a permanent family with all the love of Jesus that goes with it.

Ask any child at the Galilean Home. They may say it in different ways but they'll tell you Jerry and Sandy are real people. That there is faith, hope and room for one more at the Galilean Home.

Where the love of Christ abounds.

_ *Larry Troxell*
November, 1989

Clip, fill out the following, and mail to:

GALILEAN HOME MINISTRIES, INC.
P.O. BOX 880
LIBERTY, KENTUCKY 42539-0880
606-787-5120

_ I want to be saved from my sins.
_ Please send me the Galilean Home newsletter,
  The Shepherd.
_ Please send me information on the children's music
  tapes.
_ I want to visit the Galilean Home.
_ I would like for the Galilean Home children to present
  their program at my church or organization.
_ I am enclosing a tax deductible gift of $_____ .

NAME _____
ADDRESS _____
CITY_____
STATE_____
ZIP _____